WOODWORKING PROJECTS III

46 Easy-to-Make Projects

A Shopsmith®/Rodale Press Publication

Shopsmith®, Inc.
3931 Image Drive
Dayton, Ohio 45414-2591

Rodale Press, Inc.
33 East Minor Street
Emmaus, Pennsylvania 18098

RODALE

Preface

This book contains forty-six woodworking project plans from back issues of HANDS ON, The Home Workshop Magazine published by Shopsmith, Inc., Pete Prlain's *How-to with Wood*, and Simpson's *Book of Wood/Could* projects.

These easy-to-make projects are sure to provide any woodworker, from beginner to expert, with hours of fun and enjoyment in the shop. Many of the projects are ideal gifts for family or friends, and they are suitable for most any occasion—Christmas, birthdays, weddings.

Note that some of the projects were designed to be made using a Shopsmith router arm; these are designated by the symbol [RA] . Feel free to revise the procedures as needed to do the projects with a conventional router setup. Special woodworking techniques have been referred to in *Power Tool Woodworking for Everyone* by R. J. DeCristoforo, Reston Publishing Company.

Our thanks go out to the many readers who have contributed their project ideas over the years. Their ideas continue to provide inspiration and enjoyment for their fellow woodworkers.

A final note: As with any woodworking endeavor, always keep safety your top priority when undertaking these projects. Plan your work carefully before you begin, and always use the recommended tools and procedures. Be sure to study every project plan thoroughly, including the diagrams and list of materials, before making any cuts.

Library of Congress Cataloging-in-Publication Data
Woodworking projects.

Includes indexes.
Contents: (1) 60 easy-to-make projects from Hands on magazine—(etc.)—3. 46 easy-to-make projects—4. 49 easy-to-make projects.
1. Woodwork.   I. Shopsmith, Inc.   II. Hands on! (Dayton, Ohio).
TT180.W66   1986   684'.08   85-29792
ISBN 0-87857-618-5 (vol. 1 hardcover)
ISBN 0-87857-615-0 (vol. 1 paperback)

ISBN 0-87857-783-1 (hardcover)
ISBN 0-87857-779-3 (paperback)

Printed in the United States of America on recycled paper containing a high percentage of de-inked fiber.

Rodale Press Edition

1988
10 9 8 7 6 5 4 3 2   hardcover
10 9 8 7 6 5 4 3 2   paperback

Publisher: Shopsmith®, Inc/Rodale Press, Inc.
Text Preparation: Scharff Associates, Ltd.
Cover Photography: Mitchell T. Mandel

Contents

ACCENTS AND ACCESSORIES

TOYS AND GAMES

INDOOR PROJECTS

Accents and Accessories

From bedroom to kitchen, from TV room to dining room, the projects in this section will enhance your entire home. We've designed them to be as practical as they are attractive, and you're sure to enjoy building them as much as your family will enjoy using them.

MAGAZINE RACK

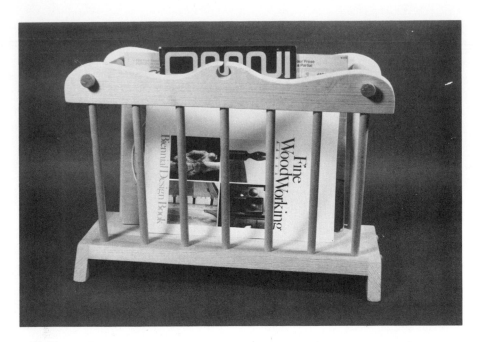

What better place to store your periodicals than in this inexpensive magazine rack? Using standard size hardwood dowels and scrap wood left over from other projects, you can build it in no time at all.

1. Sand all stock with 100-grit paper to remove mill marks.

2. Mark the location of all holes to be drilled. The fourteen 1/2"-diameter column holes in the base (A) and the four 3/4"-diameter brace holes in the rails (C) must be drilled at 10° angles.

3. Change the drill press table back to 90° to drill the fourteen 1/2"-diameter column holes and the 3/4"-diameter decorative holes in the top rails.

4. Using the patterns provided, cut the contours of the top rails and the feet (B).

5. With a handsaw or table saw, cut a 60° bevel on the edges of the base and the ends of the feet. Make sure the pieces are exactly the same width and the same angle where they join.

6. Cut the braces (D) and columns (E) to length, making sure to knock off any burrs on the ends.

7. To assemble, first attach the feet to the base using glue and #8 × 1-1/2" flathead wood screws. Countersink the screws.

8. To complete the rack assembly, use glue to fasten the ends of the columns and braces. Be sure to wipe off any excess glue immediately with a damp rag.

9. Use a sanding block to round over all sharp edges, including the protruding ends of the braces, and to smooth the joints between the base and legs.

10. Stain the rack with an Early American stain. Natural oil is recommended for the finish.

LIST OF MATERIALS

(finished dimensions in inches)

A	Base	3/4 × 7 × 16-1/2
B	Feet (2)	3/4 × 2 × 8-3/8
C	Rails (2)	3/4 × 2-1/2 × 18
D	Braces (2)	3/4-dia. × 9-3/4 dowels
E	Columns (14)	1/2-dia. × 10-1/2 dowels
	Flathead wood screws	#8 × 1-1/2
	Wood glue	

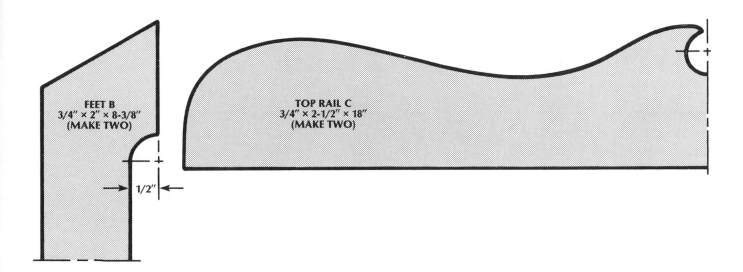

FEET B
3/4″ × 2″ × 8-3/8″
(MAKE TWO)

1/2″

TOP RAIL C
3/4″ × 2-1/2″ × 18″
(MAKE TWO)

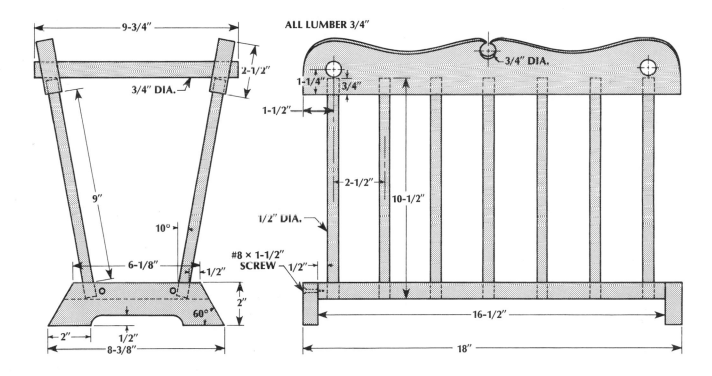

9-3/4″

2-1/2″

3/4″ DIA.

9″

10°

6-1/8″

1/2″

#8 × 1-1/2″
SCREW

2″

60°

2″

1/2″

8-3/8″

ALL LUMBER 3/4″

3/4″ DIA.

1-1/4″

3/4″

1-1/2″

2-1/2″

10-1/2″

1/2″ DIA.

1/2″

16-1/2″

18″

This recipe box can hold more than recipe cards—buttons, address cards, candy, crayons, almost any little thing around the house can find a home in it.

1. If you are unable to purchase the 1/2" stock needed for the recipe box, custom plane the necessary amount of 3/4" stock or resaw it on a bandsaw.

2. Cut the basic box parts (A, B, C, D, E) to the dimensions found in the materials list with the grain running the way indicated in the drawings. Rip a 70° bevel on the upper edges of the front, back, and top pieces and make 70° angled cuts across the upper ends of the sides.

3. Make a simple jig to hold the top and back pieces at a 70° angle while you make the cutouts for the hinge. The jig consists of a 2 × 4 with a beveled front face (see the jig layout end view) that is fastened to a table saw miter gauge with counterbored carriage bolts and wing nuts. The jig must be long enough to be used on either side of the saw blade. (A 12" length should suffice for most saws.)

4. Cut the notches on the top and back pieces with your saw blade (or dado blades, if you have them) set to a height of 9/16". Hold each piece firmly against the jig and keep its beveled edge flush with the table top while cutting. Make the notch at the center of the top piece wide enough to create 1/64"

of clearance on either side where the two pieces fit together.

5. Fit the top and back pieces together with their faces flush and a 1/16"-thick spacer holding them slightly apart. Center and drill 1/4"-diameter holes through each wing of the top piece 1" deep into the adjacent part of the back piece. This process is best done with a horizontal boring machine while the prices are held flat on a table top and against a fence.

6. Cut a 1/2" radius on the hinge sections of the top and back. Sand one end of each dowel so that it will rotate easily when fit inside the back.

7. Dry assemble the top and back to make sure the dowels fit and the hinge operates properly. Sand parts as needed.

8. If desired, cut a scallop in the inside edge of the front to make it easier to get to the front cards.

9. Glue the box together without the top. Keep excess glue off the visible parts and clamp until the glue dries.

10. Set the top in place lining up its dowel holes with those of the back. Push the dowels through the holes in the top until they barely penetrate the back. Apply glue on the last 3/4" of each dowel, then push them the rest of the way in until they are flush with the sides of the top.

11. Give the box a final touch up with sandpaper, then finish as desired. Attach the knob and mount felt pads on the upper edge of the front.

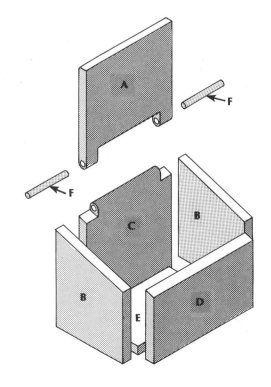

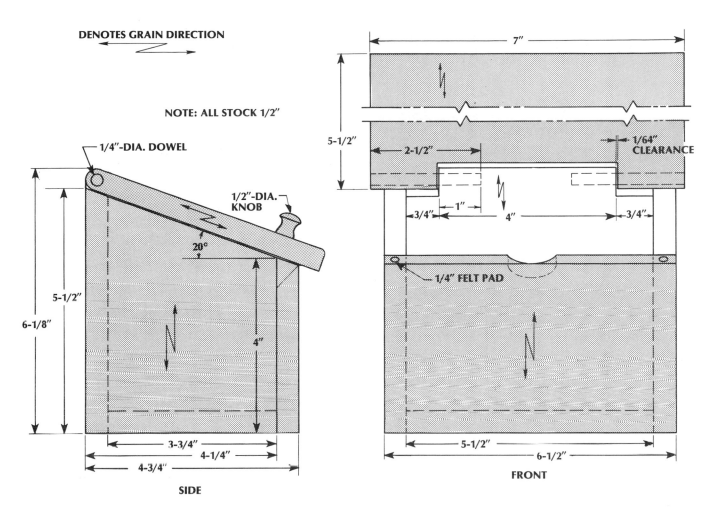

DENOTES GRAIN DIRECTION

NOTE: ALL STOCK 1/2"

1/4"-DIA. DOWEL

1/2"-DIA. KNOB

20°

6-1/8"

5-1/2"

4"

3-3/4"

4-1/4"

4-3/4"

SIDE

7"

5-1/2"

2-1/2"

1/64" CLEARANCE

3/4"

1"

4"

3/4"

1/4" FELT PAD

5-1/2"

6-1/2"

FRONT

3/4"-DIA. COUNTERBORE 1/2" DEPTH

12"

20°

3-1/2"

1-1/2"

SAWING JIG LAYOUT

LIST OF MATERIALS

(finished dimensions in inches)

A	Top	1/2 × 7 × 5-1/2
B	Sides (2)	1/2 × 4-1/4 × 5-1/2
C	Back	1/2 × 5-1/2 × 6-1/8
D	Front	1/2 × 6-1/2 × 4
E	Bottom	1/2 × 3-3/4 × 5-1/2
F	Dowels (2)	1/4 dia. × 2-1/2
	Felt pad (2)	
	Knob (optional)	
	Carriage bolts	
	Wing nuts	
	Wood glue	

This candelabra will add a touch of elegance to most any table or room. The attractive centerpiece holds three candles, making it just right for a quiet candlelight dinner or for emergency lighting.

1. Cut all pieces to size according to the dimensions given. The triangular center post (A) can either be cut from a solid piece of wood or from glued-up stock. In the latter case, it is a good idea to make some of the 60° beveled cuts prior to gluing up the material and finishing the job with a hand plane and belt sander. Flatten the sharp corners of the post with a sander or block plane.

2. Cut out the arms (B) on a bandsaw, then sand the edges smooth with a drum sander.

3. Drill matching sets of 3/8"-diameter holes 9/16" deep into the center post and the inside edge of each arm for doweling the pieces together. Center the middle hole along the length of each piece and space the remaining holes 2-1/2" apart as shown.

4. Glue the sides (C) to the arms, keeping their outer edges flush. After the glue has dried, sand the assembled arms.

5. Center and drill a 7/8"-diameter hole 1-1/4" deep in the top of each arm to hold a candle. Chamfer the edges of the holes with a 1"-diameter countersink or by hand sanding; this will allow the candles to fit in more easily.

6. Attach the arms to the center post using glue and dowels (D). Clamp until the glue has dried.

7. Finish the candelabra as desired. Glue felt pads to the bottoms of the arms to prevent furniture from being scratched.

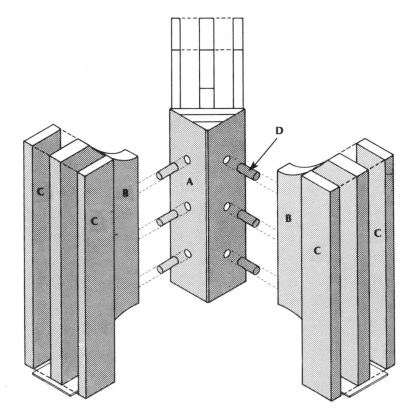

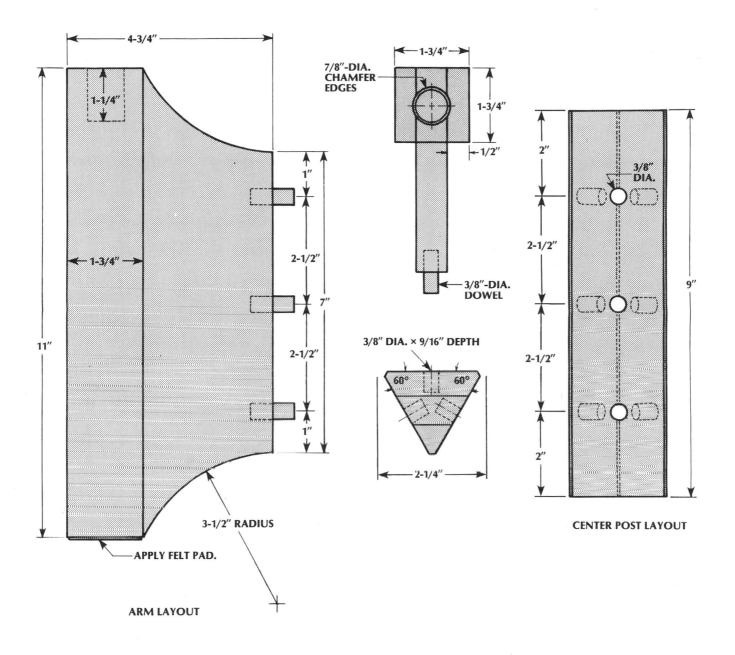

4-3/4"

1-1/4"

1-3/4"

11"

1"

2-1/2"

7"

2-1/2"

1"

3-1/2" RADIUS

APPLY FELT PAD.

ARM LAYOUT

1-3/4"

7/8"-DIA.
CHAMFER
EDGES

1-3/4"

1/2"

3/8"-DIA.
DOWEL

3/8" DIA. × 9/16" DEPTH

60°   60°

2-1/4"

3/8"
DIA.

2"

2-1/2"

2-1/2"

2"

9"

CENTER POST LAYOUT

LIST OF MATERIALS

(finished dimensions in inches)

A	Center post	2-1/4 × 2-1/4 × 2-1/4 × 9
B	Arms (3)	3/4 × 4-3/4 × 11
C	Sides (6)	1/2 × 1-3/4 × 11
D	Dowels (9)	3/8 dia. × 1
	Felt pads (3)	1-3/4 × 1-3/4
	Wood glue	

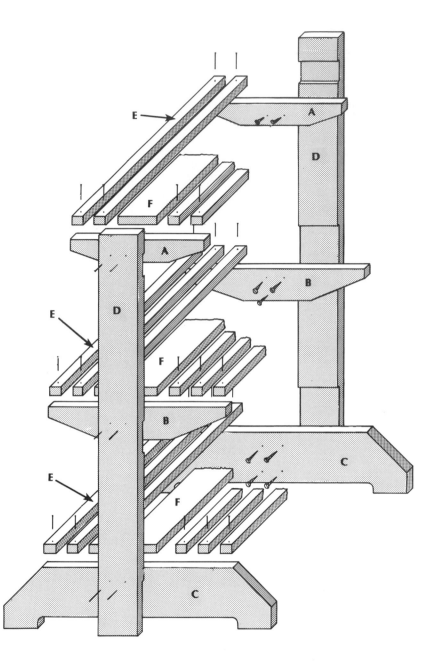

Here's the perfect alternative to crowding potted plants in your window sills: the plant display. This project has three shelves that are slatted to allow more sunlight to reach the plants on the lower shelves.

1. Begin with ten feet of 1 × 12 lumber. Use redwood, cedar, or pressure-treated lumber if the display is intended for outdoor use.

2. Cut all pieces to size on a table saw.

3. Lay out and mark the various angles on the ends of the top shelf sides (A), middle shelf sides (B), and the base pieces (C). Cut these angles using a bandsaw and 1/4" blade.

4. Using a router or a saw fitted with dado blades, cut 1/8"-deep dadoes and rabbets in the posts (D) for the shelf sides and base pieces.

5. Drill screw holes in the shelf sides and the base pieces, and corresponding pilot holes in the posts.

LIST OF MATERIALS

(finished dimensions in inches)

A	Top shelf sides (2)	3/4 × 2 × 12
B	Middle shelf sides (2)	3/4 × 3 × 16
C	Base pieces (2)	3/4 × 5-1/2 × 24
D	Posts (2)	3/4 × 3-1/2 × 36
E	Shelf slats (16)	3/4 × 1 × 18
F	Shelf center pieces(3)	3/4 × 3-1/2 × 17-3/4
	Flathead wood screws	#8 × 1-1/4
	6d finishing nails	

Drill pilot holes in the shelf slats (E) and center pieces (F) to accommodate 6d finishing nails. (Use one of the nails as a drill bit to assure that the diameter of the pilot holes is drilled accurately.)

6. Sand all of the pieces smooth. The sawed edges should be given an extra sanding, or be touched up with a hand plane, to make sure they are sufficiently smooth.

7. Attach the slats and shelf center pieces to the sides with 6d finishing nails. Attach the centers first, and then install the slats at 1" intervals. Set all nails below the surface and fill the holes with wood putty that matches the finish you plan to use.

8. Attach the shelves to the posts using #8 × 1-1/4" flathead wood screws.

9. Finish the plant display with polyurethane or some other water-resistant finish if it is not made of redwood, cedar, or pressure-treated lumber.

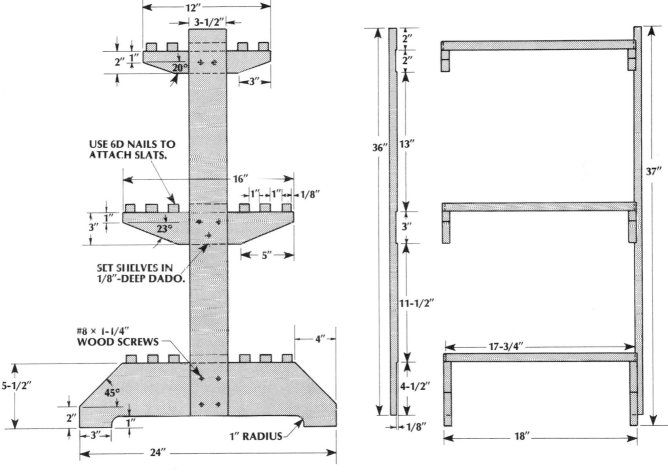

PLANT DISPLAY

If you've ever scorched a table or countertop with a hot container, you know the value of trivets in the kitchen. This popular item usually comes in three sizes: 4" × 4", 6" × 6", and 8" × 8". The technique used involves making multi-intersecting decorative cuts, similar to what is done on larger projects such as door panels and room dividers. To do this, you will need a simple fixture and a table saw or router arm, such as the homeowner model made by Shopsmith.

MAKING THE FIXTURE

The purpose of the fixture is to make straight, accurate cuts while holding the blanks securely in place. Construction of the fixture varies, depending on whether a table saw or router arm will be used to make the trivets.

1. Cut the fixture pieces to the dimensions given. If making a router arm fixture, a back brace (D) is needed; if making a table saw fixture, omit the back brace.

2. Cut the sliding dovetail in the extension bar (A) and the cradle (B). Check the fit—it must slide smoothly.

3. Place the extension bar and cradle on the table saw or router arm table, lining up the center of the cradle V-notch with the cutter. Mark a centerline on the cradle and extension bar, then mark one inch increments on both sides of the centerline.

4. On the router arm fixture, center and drill 1/4"-diameter indexing holes 3/8" deep into the back edge of the cradle; drill matching holes through the back brace and the extension bar. On the table saw fixture, drill a 1/4"-diameter hole down from the upper edge 2-1/4" deep into the extension bar. Center the hole 1/4" from the front face and at the point along the length of the extension bar that is directly in line with the saw's dado blades. Make indexing notches in

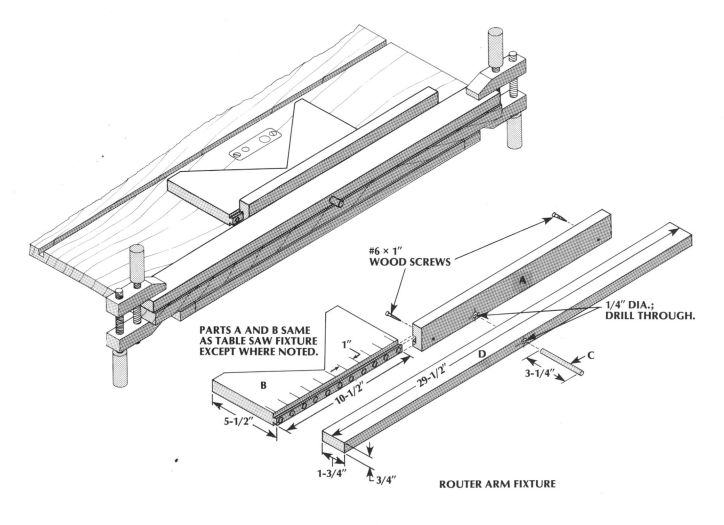

#6 × 1"
WOOD SCREWS

PARTS A AND B SAME
AS TABLE SAW FIXTURE
EXCEPT WHERE NOTED.

1"

B

5-1/2"

10-1/2"

29-1/2"

D

3-1/4"

C

A

1/4" DIA.;
DRILL THROUGH.

1-3/4"

3/4"

ROUTER ARM FIXTURE

the back edge of the cradle by sliding it along the slot in the extension bar and drilling through the hole in the bar.

5. Clamp the router arm fixture on the saw table. For the table saw fixture, drill two holes in the extension bar and attach it to the miter gauge with carriage bolts and wing nuts.

MAKING THE TRIVETS

Trivets utilize 3/4"-thick stock cut into blanks of 4" × 4", 6" × 6", and 8" × 8". Only one blank at a time can be inserted into the fixture and cut.

1. If using a table saw, set dado blades to cut a 1/2" kerf. If using a router arm, use a carbide-tipped straight router bit or any decorative bit without a pilot.

2. All cuts are 1/2" deep. Start at one corner, make the first cut, then rotate the blank 180° and cut across the other corner.

3. Remove the stop pin (C), then slide in the cradle and blank one

inch. Reinsert the pin and cut the next groove. As before, turn the blank 180° and cut the second groove on the other side. Continue in this manner until you reach the middle of the blank and the top is completed.

4. Turn the blank over, rotate it 90°, and begin the same cutting procedure from corner to middle.

5. Sand the edges of the trivets with a disc sander. For overall sanding, use flutter sheets. Use a good heat- and water-resistant finish.

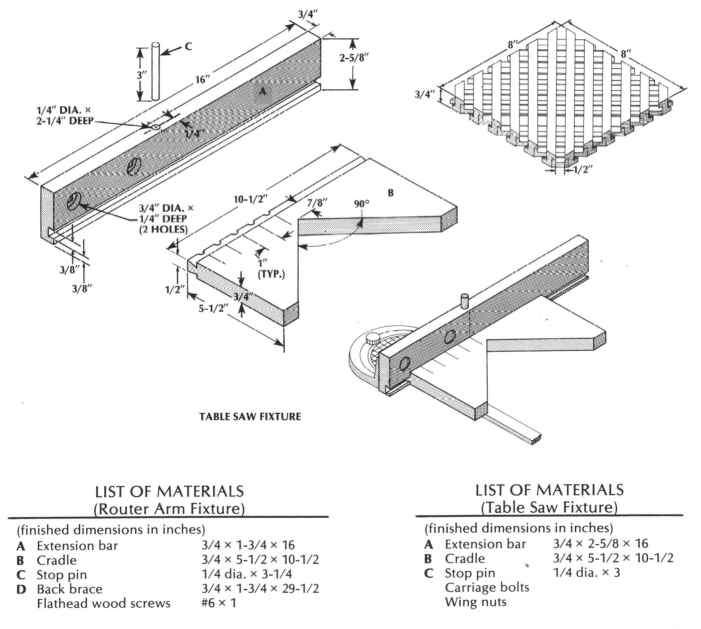

TABLE SAW FIXTURE

LIST OF MATERIALS
(Router Arm Fixture)

(finished dimensions in inches)

A	Extension bar	3/4 × 1-3/4 × 16
B	Cradle	3/4 × 5-1/2 × 10-1/2
C	Stop pin	1/4 dia. × 3-1/4
D	Back brace	3/4 × 1-3/4 × 29-1/2
	Flathead wood screws	#6 × 1

LIST OF MATERIALS
(Table Saw Fixture)

(finished dimensions in inches)

A	Extension bar	3/4 × 2-5/8 × 16
B	Cradle	3/4 × 5-1/2 × 10-1/2
C	Stop pin	1/4 dia. × 3
	Carriage bolts	
	Wing nuts	

Pocket watches are a beautiful link to the past, and this watch keep is ideal for displaying these old treasures.

1. This project is constructed of 1 × 4 stock and 1/4″-radius quarter-round molding. The material used for the cabinet sides (B) and back (C) and the door stiles (D) and rails (E) must be planed or resawn and sanded down to 1/2″ thickness.

2. Begin by edge-gluing two 9″ lengths of 3/4″ stock to serve as the basis for the back panel. After the glue has dried on the panel, cut all the parts for the cabinet case and door to the finished dimensions.

3. Using a table saw, router, or hand plane, cut a 45° chamfer on the front and side edges of the top and bottom pieces (A).

4. Sand all of the cabinet and door pieces. Drill the dowel holes according to the diagram, using a horizontal boring machine or a doweling jig and hand-held drill.

5. Assemble the door and cabinet (without the back) as two separate units and make sure they are

1/4″-DIA. × 1″
DOWELS
(12 REQUIRED)

A

B

C

B

A

H

D

F

B

F

G

G

E

D

5/8″ BRADS
(8 REQUIRED)

square. Clamp them together until the glue dries.

6. Rout a 1/4"-wide × 1/4"-deep rabbet in the back of the door, using a straight router bit. Square the corners using a hand chisel.

7. Cut a 1/4"-deep × 1/2"-wide × 6"-long stop rabbet in the back edge of both the top and bottom cabinet pieces.

8. Prior to installing the back, drill 1/8"-diameter holes in the back for the hanging pegs. Drill the holes at a 5° slant to the depth of 3/8". If using wooden pegs, install them; if using brass rods, wait until after finishing the watch keep to install them.

9. Nail and glue the back into the cabinet. Miter the ends of the glass retainer molding (F, G) for the door while you wait for the glue to dry.

10. If necessary, sand the top and bottom of the door to prevent

LIST OF MATERIALS

(finished dimensions in inches)

A	Top and bottom (2)	3/4 × 3 × 8
B	Sides (2)	1/2 × 2 × 8
C	Back	1/2 × 6 × 8-1/2
D	Door stiles (2)	1/2 × 1 × 8
E	Door rails (2)	1/2 × 1 × 5
F	Side glass retainers (2)	1/4 × 1/4 × 6-1/2
G	Top & bottom glass retainers (2)	1/4 × 1/4 × 5-1/2
H	Dowels (12)	1-1/4 dia. × 1
	Knob	1/2 dia.
	Hanging pegs (4)	1/8 dia. × 1-1/8
	Glass	1/8 × 5-3/8 × 6-3/8
	Brads	#18 × 5/8
	Hinge with screws (pair)	
	Door latch	
	Wood glue	

them from rubbing or binding. Sand the sides so they fit flush with the cabinet.

11. Finish all the pieces, including the quarter-round glass retainers.

12. Install the glass with the glass retainers. Drill holes in the retain-

ers for brads, then attach the retainers with brads.

13. If using brass hanging pegs, install them now.

14. Install the hinges with screws to mount the door. Install the knob and latch to complete the keep.

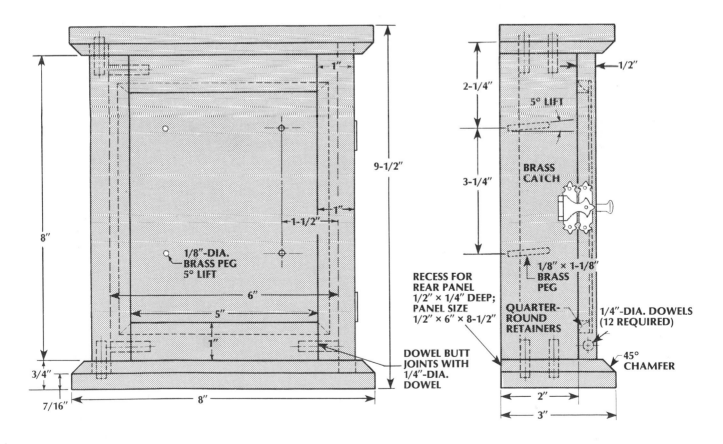

HANGING WINE GLASS RACK

With this decorative hanging rack you can show off your fine wine glasses. It's useful in any kitchen or above any bar; it is attractive, and also helps solve your storage problems.

1. To make the wine glass rack, start with a 38" length of 2 × 4, a 49" length of 1 × 8, and two dowel rods (one 1/4" in diameter and one 3/4" in diameter).

2. Crosscut the 2 × 4 into two 18-1/2"-long pieces. Rip, then plane or sand these pieces to a thickness of 1-1/4" and a width of 2-1/2" to make the crosspieces (A).

3. Crosscut the 3/4"-thick stock into 24"-long boards, then rip these boards into 3-1/2"-wide pieces for the rails (B).

4. Cut the 3/4"-diameter dowel rod (C1) into eight 5"-long pieces. Cut the 1/4"-diameter dowel rod (C2) into eight 1-1/4"-long pieces. To make sure that the pieces are the same length, use a stop block when crosscutting.

5. Clamp the adjacent rails together two at a time to drill the glass stem recesses. From the ends, measure in 3" and mark a point. From these marks, space the other recesses 4-1/2" apart. Using a countersink bit, drill a 1/4"-deep recess where the edges of the rails meet.

6. Mark the centerpoints for the screw eye and dowel holes in the upper edge of the crosspieces. Center the screw eye holes 1-1/2" in from each end and the dowel holes

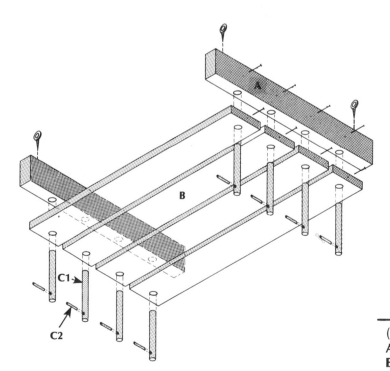

LIST OF MATERIALS

(finished dimensions in inches)

A	Crosspieces (2)	1-1/4 × 2-1/2 × 18-1/2
B	Rails (4)	3/4 × 3-1/2 × 24
C1	Dowels (8)	3/4 dia. × 5
C2	Dowels (8)	1/4 dia. × 1-1/4
	Screw eyes (4)	1 dia. × 2-1/4
	Brads	#16 × 1-1/4
	Wood glue	

3-1/4" in from the ends and 4" apart. Mark the dowel hole centers 1" from the ends and midway across the lower faces on the rails.

7. Drill pilot holes for the screw eyes 1" deep into the crosspieces. Drill 3/4"-diameter dowel holes completely through the crosspieces and the rails. To avoid tearout when drilling the dowel holes, drill only until the tip of the bit penetrates the far side of each piece, then flip the piece over to complete the hole.

8. Center and drill a 1/4"-diameter hole through each 3/4"-diameter dowel 5/8" from one end. Hold the dowels steady for drilling by placing them in a V-groove plowed down the middle of a block of scrap lumber. Position the block so that the drill bit will strike the center of the groove, then clamp it to the table or hold it firmly against a fence.

9. Sand all pieces before assembling.

10. Drive the 1/4"-diameter dowels through the ends of the larger dowels so that their ends extend the same distance to either side. Then fit the rails onto the larger dowels and push them down until they are stopped by the smaller dowels.

11. Make sure the rails are turned so that the tapered recesses on their edges will face up when the unit is installed. Then drive brads through the ends of the rails into the dowels to prevent them from moving out of position.

12. Arrange the rails so that the two with recesses on both edges are in the middle and the recessed edges of the other two face inside.

Spread glue inside the dowel holes in the crosspieces and the upper ends of the dowels. Then insert the dowels into the underside of the crosspieces, pushing them up until their upper ends barely emerge from the crosspieces. After the glue dries, sand the dowel ends flush with the crosspieces.

13. If you want to stain the assembly, do it at this time, then rub with steel wool.

14. Finally, install the screw eyes and hang the rack.

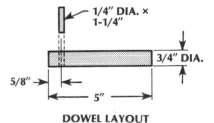

DOWEL LAYOUT

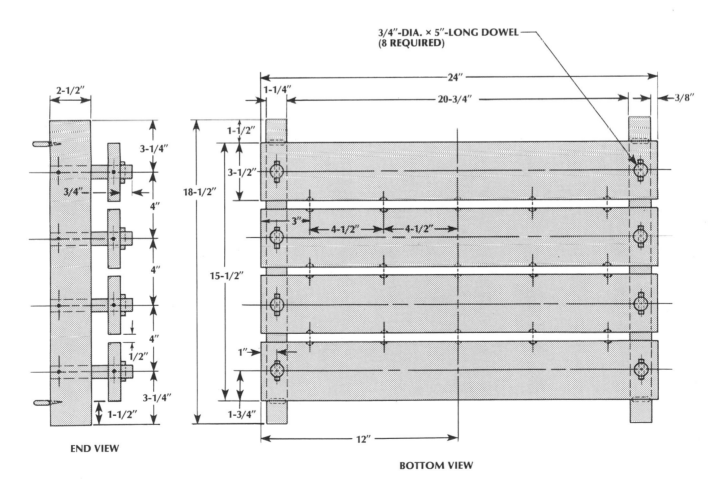

3/4"-DIA. × 5"-LONG DOWEL
(8 REQUIRED)

END VIEW

BOTTOM VIEW

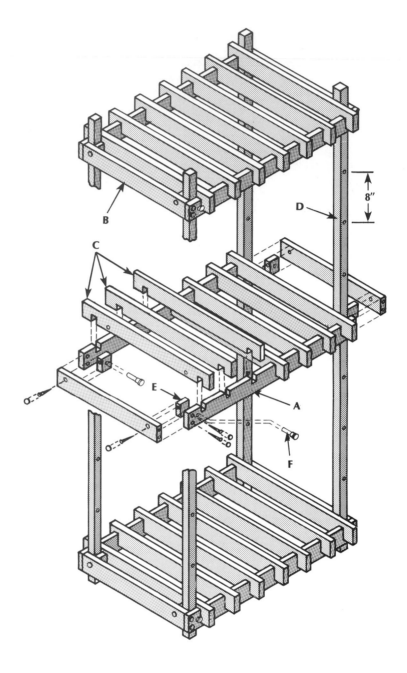

Nothing brightens up a home better than a hanging plant. If you have a south-facing window or glass doors, you can bring your garden indoors for the winter with these attractive adjustable plant shelves. The shelves are slatted rather than solid so that the plants on the bottom can receive more light. If you build the shelves with cedar, redwood, or other weather-resistant lumber, you can keep the shelves outdoors during the summer.

1. Begin by measuring the window or door opening next to which you will place the shelves, and adjust the dimensions of the materials as needed. Keep in mind that the total unit should be no higher or wider than the window or door.

2. Begin construction of the shelves by cutting the front and back frames (A), side frames (B),

LIST OF MATERIALS

(finished dimensions in inches)

A	Front and back frames (6)	3/4 × 2-1/2 × 30
B	Side frames (6)	3/4 × 2-1/2 × 17
C	Slats (21)	3/4 × 2-1/2 × 21-1/2
D	Stiles (4)	1-1/2 × 1-1/2 × 72
E	Peg blocks (12)	3/4 × 2 × 1-1/2
F	Pegs (12)	1 dia. × 2-1/2
	Dowel buttons (36)	3/8 dia.
	Flathead wood screws	#10 × 1-1/2
	Waterproof glue	

slats (C), and peg blocks (E) to size from 1 × 3 stock.

3. The slats and the front and back frame members are joined together using cross lap joints as shown in the exploded-view drawing. These joints are formed by cutting 3/4"-wide dadoes 1" deep in both sets of pieces.

4. Lay out and cut the dadoes on the front and back frames as shown in the front frame and shelf layout drawings. Note that the middle dado is centered along the length of the frames and that all dadoes are 3-3/8" apart.

5. Lay out and cut a pair of dadoes on each slat as shown in the slat detail drawing. Note that these dadoes are set 1-1/2" from the ends of the pieces.

6. Drill 1/2"-diameter peg holes through the front frames and back peg blocks. The holes in the front frames are centered 1" below the upper edge and 1-1/2" from each end. The holes in the blocks are centered on both width and length. Counterbore screw holes in the front and back frames, side frames, and the outermost slats of each shelf. Then sand all the shelf pieces.

7. Assemble the frames, using waterproof glue and #10 × 1-1/2" flathead wood screws. Do not glue in the five middle slats of the top shelf; with these slats left unglued and detachable it is much easier to put up and take down your plants.

8. Cover the counterbored screws with 3/8"-diameter dowel buttons.

9. Cut the four stiles (D) from 2 × 2 stock. Center and drill 1/2"-diameter peg holes at 8" intervals along the length of each stile, beginning 4" from either end. Sand the stiles.

10. Turn the pegs (F) on a lathe from scrap 2 × 2 stock to the profile shown in the peg detail. Sand and finish the pegs on the lathe.

11. If you are planning to use the shelves outdoors, finish with a good outdoor finish such as spar varnish or polyurethane. (If you used cedar, redwood, or weather-resistant lumber, no finish is necessary.)

12. Finish the assembly by sliding the shelves over the ends of the stiles. Position the shelves and secure them with the pegs.

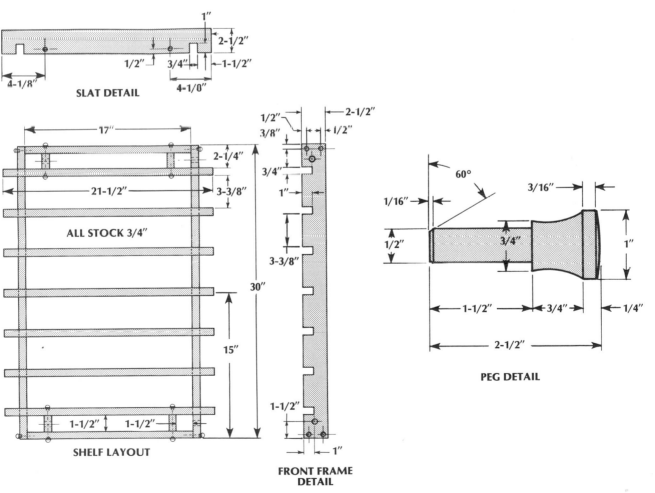

SLAT DETAIL

SHELF LAYOUT

ALL STOCK 3/4"

FRONT FRAME DETAIL

PEG DETAIL

CORNER UMBRELLA STAND

Set the grooves 1/2" back of the radiused edges of the pieces.

3. Rout a 1/8"-wide × 1/4"-deep dado across each side piece (B) 3/8" in from the front edge to receive the ends of the front panel.

4. Lay out and cut nine 2-1/2"-diameter holes in the top, arranged as shown in the drawing. Sand the edges of the holes and any other rough edges on any of the pieces.

5. Dry assemble the stand to check the fit. Keep the outside faces of the sides flush with the straight edges of the top and bottom. Trim one end of the front panel if necessary to get a good fit.

6. Run a bead of glue inside the grooves and dadoes and along all edges where parts will join. Assemble the stand, using 4d finishing nails to fasten the top and bottom to the sides while the glue dries.

7. Finish the stand with two coats of latex paint.

The umbrella stand described here was built of particleboard and hardboard, then covered with white latex paint. The hardboard is the ideal choice for the front because it bends easily. However, the other parts can be made of waferboard or plywood, if you prefer.

1. Cut the pieces to size according to the dimensions given.

2. Lay out and cut an 18-1/2" radius across the front corner of the top and bottom pieces (C). Then rout a 1/8"-wide × 1/4"-deep groove in each piece to receive the front (A).

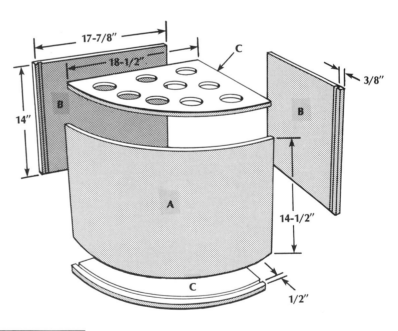

LIST OF MATERIALS

(finished dimensions in inches)

A	Front	1/8 × 14-1/2 × 28-1/2 hardboard
B	Sides (2)	1/2 × 14 × 17-7/8 particleboard
C	Top and bottom	1/2 × 18-1/2 × 18-1/2 particleboard
	4d finishing nails	
	Wood glue	
	Latex paint	

A brightly colored, round ceramic tile makes the perfect working surface for this wooden cutting board. As an added attraction, the wire bladed knife is designed to fit right into the board, so it's at your fingertips when you need it.

1. The cutting board is made from two 7" × 11" pieces of maple or cherry. Begin the project by resawing or planing both boards to 5/16" in thickness and trimming them to the overall shape shown in the drawing.

2. Leave one board whole to serve as the base. Cut the knife handle, the two knife holders, and the opening for the tile out of the other piece following the instructions given in the drawings. Adapt the dimensions as needed to fit the precise dimensions of your ceramic tile.

3. Since the pieces cut out of the knife handle are used as the knife holders, the cuts must be made with minimal waste. Begin by drilling a tiny hole through the piece on one cutting line and slipping a jeweler's blade through. Then fasten the blade in a scroll saw and complete the cut.

4. Use glue to fasten the tile holder and knife holder pieces to the cutting board base, clamping the pieces until the glue dries. Use the knife handle to properly position the knife holder pieces, but be careful not to accidentally glue it in place.

5. When the glue has set, sand the cutting board and knife handle with fine sandpaper to round all sharp corners.

6. Use an unwound steel musical instrument string for the knife blade. Drill holes for the wire diagonally through the tips of the knife handle to minimize chances of the wood splitting when the wire is tensioned. Counterbore the outside ends of the holes slightly to make room for the anchor on one end of the string and the knot on the other end.

7. Stain if desired, then apply one or two coats of polyurethane or penetrating oil finish for protection.

8. Attach three small tack feet to the bottom of the cutting board to prevent it from sliding when in use. Install the tile, and the board is ready for use.

LIST OF MATERIALS

(finished dimensions in inches)

A	Cutting board blanks (2)	5/16 × 7 × 11
	Ceramic tile	3/8 × 6 dia.
	Steel wire	
	Tack feet	
	Fine sandpaper	
	Wood glue	

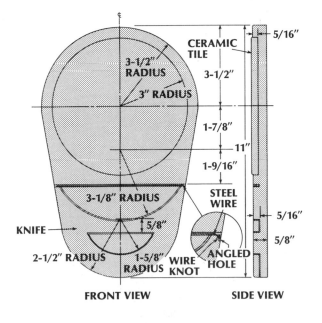

FRONT VIEW   SIDE VIEW

This lantern-style lamp and shoji screen can be used indoors or out. It's constructed easily with glue and small brads; however, remember to nail carefully to avoid splitting the wood.

1. After cutting all the pieces to size, assemble the frames by attaching the rails (B) to the legs (A) with dowels and glue. Place the rails 3/4" down from the tops of the legs and 6-3/8" up from the bottoms as shown.

2. Rout a 6-1/4"-long channel up the center of one of the legs, beginning at the bottom. Make the channel wide and deep enough to enclose the lamp cord and place it on an outside edge that can be covered by an overlapping frame as shown in the drawing. Then, on the adjacent inside face of the leg, drill a hole that intersects the upper end of the channel to provide an exit for the cord. Pick the frame that will cover the cord channel and drill a hole through it near the bottom of the appropriate leg to provide an entry path for the cord.

3. Dry fit the four frames, mark them, and drill holes for doweling them together. Then sand and finish the frames as desired.

4. Cut a piece of fiberglass fabric large enough to cover the rectangular opening in each frame. Fasten the fiberglass panels to the inner face of each frame using small wire nails.

5. Drill a hole through the base (C), centered along its length and 1-1/2" from one side. Size the hole to accept the pipe nipple found in the lamp socket kit.

6. Fasten the base between the frame with the cord channel and one other frame using dowels and glue. Make the base side that is farthest from the pipe nipple hole flush with the outside edges on one side of the frames to create a

ventilation and access space on the other side.

7. Lace the lamp cord through the holes and channel in the two frames, pulling enough out the upper end for connecting with the socket. Fasten the four frames together using glue and dowels. Then glue and tack the support strips (D, E) to the backs of the upper rails, keeping their lower edges flush.

8. Insert the pipe nipple into the base, keeping the nut on the lower end. Run the cord up through the nipple and fasten it to the socket, then mount the socket on the nipple. Rotate the socket to place the pull chain side next to the ventilation hole, then tighten the nut.

9. Cut a piece of fiberglass to serve as the top of the lamp. Glue and tack it to the top edges of the support strips.

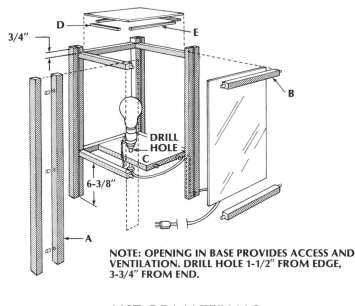

NOTE: OPENING IN BASE PROVIDES ACCESS AND VENTILATION. DRILL HOLE 1-1/2" FROM EDGE, 3-3/4" FROM END.

LIST OF MATERIALS

(finished dimensions in inches)

A	Legs (8)	3/4 × 3/4 × 24
B	Rails (8)	3/4 × 3/4 × 7-1/2
C	Base	3/4 × 6 × 7-1/2
D	Support strips (2)	5/16 × 1/2 × 7-1/2
E	Support strips (2)	5/16 × 1/2 × 8-3/8
	Dowels	3/8 dia. × 1-1/2
	Wire nails	
	Lamp socket kit	
	(socket, pull chain, cord, pipe nipple, and nut)	
	Fiberglass fabric	
	Wood glue	

Kitchen utensils have a way of getting lost just when you need them. Such confusion can be avoided by building this special holder for them.

1. Cut the rack (A) and base (B) to size.

2. Drill appropriately sized holes in the rack to accommodate large spoons and other utensils.

3. Glue and tack a piece of decorative molding to the front of the rack as shown.

4. Butt the rack against the base, or rout a shallow groove for it. Fasten them together using glue and screws inserted from behind.

5. Dress up the holder by nailing various moldings to the front, top, and bottom edges of the base. The ones used on the original are profiled below, but choose moldings to suit your own taste.

6. Finish the holder as desired, then mount it on the wall or the side of a cabinet.

LIST OF MATERIALS

(finished dimensions in inches)

A	Rack	3/4 × 3-1/2 × 12
B	Base	3/4 × 3-1/2 × 12
	Wood screws	
	Finishing nails	
	Decorative moldings	
	Wood glue	

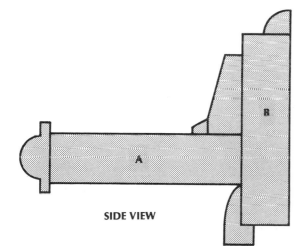

SIDE VIEW

Here's a handsome pedestal to display your favorite plant. The original was made of clear grade redwood. The wider pieces were glued up from narrower stock and custom cut to the dimensions listed.

1. Cut all of the pieces to size according to the dimensions given.

2. Cut three plug holes in each column side (A) as shown. Locate the holes 2-1/2" from each end, with the remaining hole in between. All of the holes should be centered 3/8" from one edge of the piece.

3. Drill pilot holes for the wood screws in the center of the plug holes.

4. Assemble the column by gluing and screwing one corner at a time. Be sure that the assembly is square.

5. Round the edges of the column by sanding or routing with a 1/4" radius bit.

6. Cut 45° miters at the corners of the apron pieces (G).

7. Round or bead the upper edges of the top (E), then center the apron pieces on the underside of the top. Glue and screw through the apron into the top.

8. Center the bracket (F) on the column; then glue and screw it in place. Center the top/apron assembly on the bracket; glue and screw through the bracket into the apron.

9. Round or bead the upper edges of the base pieces (B, C) and feet (D); then sand.

10. Center the small base piece on the bottom of the column. Glue and screw it in place from underneath. Repeat with the large base piece.

11. Position the feet so they extend beyond the corners of the base as shown; secure with glue and screws.

12. Sand the completed plant stand; finish as desired.

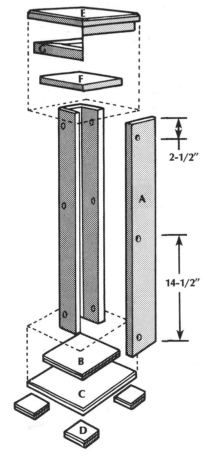

LIST OF MATERIALS

(finished dimensions in inches)

A	Column sides (4)	3/4 × 4 × 29
B	Base piece	3/4 × 7-1/2 × 7-1/2
C	Base piece	3/4 × 9-1/2 × 9-1/2
D	Feet (4)	3/4 × 3 × 3
E	Top	3/4 × 11-1/2 × 11-1/2
F	Bracket	3/4 × 7 × 7
G	Apron pieces (4)	3/4 × 3/4 × 10-1/2
	Flathead wood screws	#6 × 1-1/4
	Wood plugs	3/8 dia.
	Wood glue	

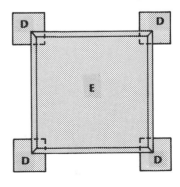

FOOT DETAIL

You'll always have a place to hang your hat with this easy-to-build hall tree. And by replacing the brass hooks with pot clips, you can turn it into a plant pole that is perfect for hanging vines. Either way, it's a useful addition to any home.

1. Begin by cutting all pieces to the listed dimensions.

2. Arrange the column sides (A) so their edges chase one another, creating a square column. Counterbore pilot holes and fasten the column sides together using wood glue and flathead wood screws. Fill the holes with wood plugs. (To avoid counterboring and plugging, use finishing nails instead of screws.) Sand the column, making the plugs flush with the other surfaces.

3. Center and drill a 5/16"-diameter hole through each column side 1-1/2" from the bottom to allow insertion of hanger bolts.

4. Lay out the final shape for the feet (B) using the template pro-vided. Drill 7/32"-diameter pilot holes for the hanger bolts in the back edge, then cut out the feet. Round over all edges except those that will meet the column.

5. Chamfer the upper edges on each of the three top pieces (C, D, E), then attach them to the bracket (F) using wood glue and finishing nails. Begin by fastening D to C, then E to D, and finally F to E. Make sure the smaller pieces are centered on the larger ones.

6. Round over the corners of the column and the sharp lower edges on the largest top piece. Spread glue on the bracket edges and fit it inside the upper end of the column.

7. Finish the tree and the feet as desired.

8. Screw the hanger bolts into the feet, then mount them on the tree, securing them with lock washers and nuts.

9. Install brass hooks and the tree is ready for your hats and coats.

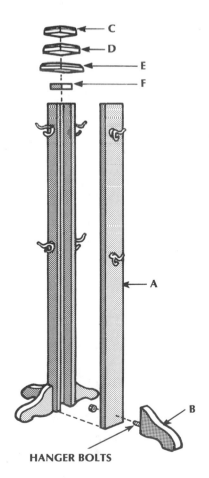

LIST OF MATERIALS

(finished dimensions in inches)

A	Column sides (4)	3/4 × 4 × 63
B	Feet (4)	1-1/2 × 5-1/2 × 8-1/2
C	Top	3/4 × 4-1/4 × 4-1/4
D	Top	3/4 × 5-3/4 × 5-3/4
E	Top	3/4 × 7-1/4 × 7-1/4
F	Bracket	3/4 × 3-1/4 × 3-1/4
	Flathead wood screws	#8 × 1-1/4
	3d finishing nails	
	Hanger bolts	1/4 dia. × 2-1/2
	Nuts and lock washers	
	Brass hooks or pot clips	
	Wood plugs	3/8 dia.
	Wood glue	

HANGER BOLT LOCATION

ONE SQUARE = 1"

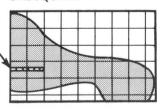

TEMPLATE FOR FEET

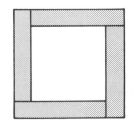

COLUMN TOP VIEW

HANGER BOLTS

Candles lend elegance and beauty to any occasion, and these attractive wooden candle stands will enhance all your candlelit moments.

1. This project is designed to be made from a 6' length of 1 × 10 with little waste of materials. A dark wood, such as walnut, is particularly nice, but pick the material you prefer.

2. Begin by cutting off a 12-1/2" length for the base (D). To minimize cupping, rip this piece into two or three pieces, square the edges, then glue the pieces back together, alternating the direction of the growth rings from piece to piece.

3. Next, cut a 33" length from the board. Rip the piece down the middle, then cut each half into three equal lengths. Face laminate the six pieces to create a blank for the large stand (A).

4. Rip a 2-1/4"-wide piece off the remainder of the board. Cut it into three equal lengths. Face laminate the three pieces to create a blank for the small stand (C).

5. Rip the rest of the board down the middle, then cut two equal lengths out of each half. Face laminate the four pieces to create a blank for the medium stand (B).

6. After the glue has dried, square up the four sides of each block. Cut the blocks to the finished dimensions in the list, then sand both ends smooth on each. Center and drill 3/8"-diameter holes 3/4" deep into the bottom of each for later mounting on the base.

7. Make full-size templates for the blocks out of stiff cardboard or thin plywood. Trace the pattern onto two adjacent sides of each block.

8. Cut the blocks to their final shape on a bandsaw. Cut carefully along the lines on one face, then tape the waste back in place, flip the block 90°, and cut along the lines on the other marked face.

9. Cut the base to its final width and length, beveling the edges in about 15° toward the upper face.

10. Arrange the stands on the base and mark their position. Center and drill 3/8"-diameter holes through the base at the appropriate points for inserting the mounting dowels (E).

11. Sand the stands and base smooth, then assemble using glue and 3/8"-diameter dowels. After the glue dries, remove any dowel protruding through the bottom of the base. Apply your choice of finish.

LIST OF MATERIALS

(finished dimensions in inches)

A	Large stand	4 × 4 × 10
B	Medium stand	3 × 3 × 8
C	Small stand	2 × 2 × 5-1/2
D	Base	3/4 × 8 × 12
E	Dowels (3)	3/8 dia. × 1-1/2
	Wood glue	

ONE SQUARE = 1/4"

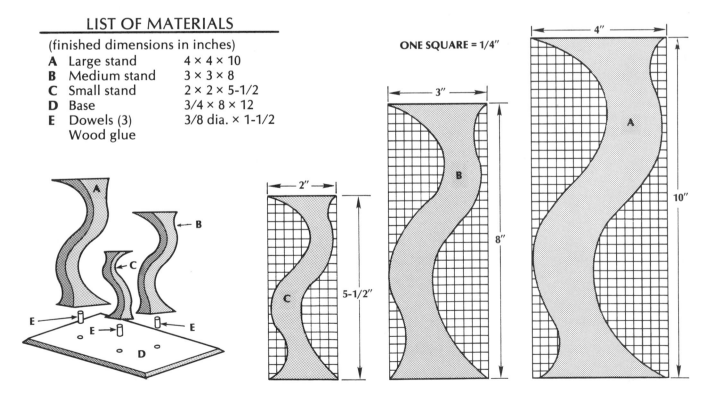

If space is a problem around your home, this handy little plant stand could be the answer. The two bottom shelves provide ample space for small and medium size plants, while the top shelf can accommodate plants of slightly larger size.

1. Cut all the pieces to size according to the dimensions given.

2. Cut a 22° bevel on each end of each leg (B) so that, when installed, the legs will slant in but their ends will remain parallel.

3. Measure from the outside edge 2" across the beveled end at the top of each leg and square a line down from that point. Cut along those lines to create the joints between legs shown in the drawing.

4. Place a pair of legs together on a flat surface and lay a brace (C) across their upper ends. Adjust the brace so that its upper edge is parallel to and 3/4" below the upper ends of the legs. Mark and trim the ends of the brace so they will be flush with the outside edges of the legs. Repeat with the other brace and pair of legs.

5. Begin the assembly of the stand by laying each pair of legs across its brace and base piece (A). Make sure the bottom edges of the legs and base are flush and that the base extends an equal distance to either side. Fasten the legs to the base and brace using water-resistant wood glue and 10d galvanized nails. If working with redwood, blunt the ends of the nails before using.

6. Set the two leg units upright and fit the shelves (D) between them.

Make sure the outer edge of each lower shelf is flush with the ends of the base and that the upper shelf is centered over the braces. Fasten the shelves in place using water-resistant wood glue and 10d galvanized nails.

7. Blunt any penetrating nail ends and break over all sharp edges. Apply a water-resistant finish.

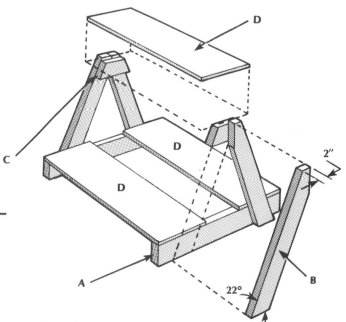

LIST OF MATERIALS

(finished dimensions in inches)

A	Base pieces (2)	1-1/2 × 3-1/2 × 22
B	Legs (4)	1-1/2 × 3-1/2 × 20
C	Braces (2)	1-1/2 × 3-1/2 × 7-1/2
D	Shelves (3)	3/4 × 7-1/4 × 30
	10d galvanized nails	
	Water-resistant wood glue	

GARDENING BENCH

The functional design of this simple bench provides comfortable seating close to the ground, so you won't have to stoop or kneel. Besides being ideal for the garden or patio, it's also a natural in the bath or shower, if redwood or special-treated wood is used.

1. After cutting all of the pieces to size, round off the ends of the two outside top pieces (C).

2. Cut a 1-1/2" × 1-1/2" notch on each end of the cross brace (B) as shown to accommodate the legs (A).

3. Cut a 4"-diameter opening and 1-1/2" × 2" slot in the bottom of each leg as shown.

4. Glue and nail the legs to the cross brace. If working with redwood, blunt the ends of the nails before using.

5. Evenly space the top pieces on the legs, and secure them with glue and nails.

6. Sand and apply the water-resistant finish of your choice.

LIST OF MATERIALS

(finished dimensions in inches)

A	Legs (2)	1-1/2 × 9-1/4 × 6
B	Cross brace	1-1/2 × 3-1/2 × 12
C	Top (6)	3/4 × 1-1/2 × 15
	Galvanized nails	
	Wood glue	

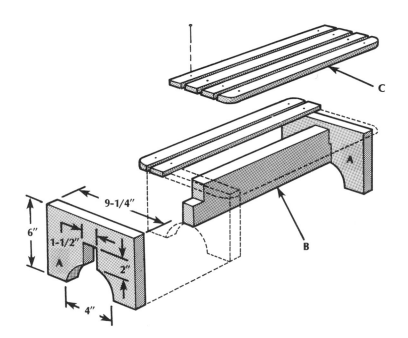

This wine bottle rack is expandable, so you can build the original three-tier module and add on later as your wine collection grows. Slotted construction enables it to go together quickly and be disassembled just as fast when it must be moved.

1. Make cardboard patterns of the front and back (A) and side pieces (B). Note that the front and back pieces have a 3/4" × 1-3/8" slot cut in each end, and three evenly spaced 3-1/4"-diameter cutouts as shown. The side pieces also have 3/4" × 1-3/8" slots cut in their ends.

2. Transfer the patterns to redwood (or any other wood of your choice), and cut as many pieces as needed for the number of tiers desired. Clamp the side pieces together to assure a uniform fit, and cut the slots on a table saw or radial arm saw. Note that the bottom edges of the bottom tier pieces and the upper edges of the top tier pieces need no slots.

3. Use a saber saw to make the round cuts on the front and back pieces. No round cuts are needed on the bottom edges of the bottom tier pieces.

4. Assemble the rack by fitting the slots together as shown. No glue or nails are required.

LIST OF MATERIALS

(finished dimensions in inches)

A	Front and back pieces (6)	3/4 × 5-1/2 × 18
B	Side pieces (4)	3/4 × 5-1/2 × 10-1/2

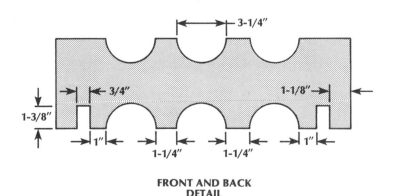

FRONT AND BACK DETAIL

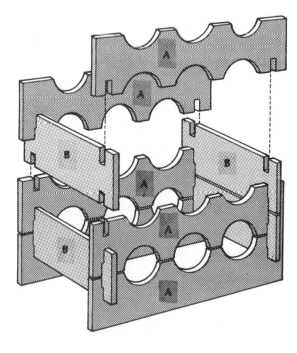

For serving everything from snacks to meals, this handsome lap tray will be a welcome addition to your kitchen. And, to complement the tray, the easy-to-make coasters are perfect. Once the coaster project is properly set up, you can make numerous sets to give as gifts.

LAP TRAY

1. Cut the various parts to size using the dimensions given.

2. Make a template for the sides (A) using the pattern provided. Use a scroll saw, bandsaw, or jigsaw to cut out the sides, then cut out the handle holes.

3. Smooth the curved surfaces with a small drum sander.

4. Using a router with a 1/4" rounding over bit, shape the top edge of the sides and the handle holes. Shape the top edge of the front (B) and back (D) as well.

5. Using a 1/4" dado head set to a depth of 1/2", cut the fingers for the box joint corners on both ends of the sides, bottom, and back.

6. Reset the dado head to a depth of 7/32", then cut the 1/4"-wide grooves in the sides, front, and back to accept the bottom (C).

7. Assemble the tray using glue in the corner joints, but leaving the bottom free to respond to movement of the other parts.

8. Sand the tray and finish as desired.

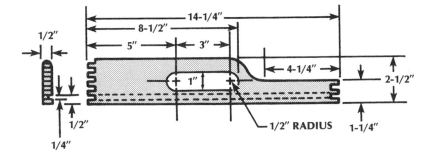

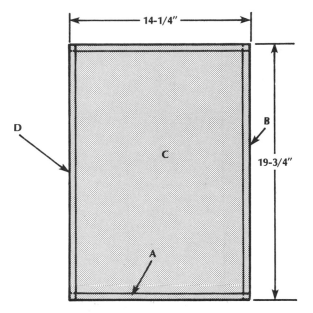

14-1/4"

19-3/4"

D

B

C

A

LIST OF MATERIALS (Lap Tray)

(finished dimensions in inches)

A	Sides (2)	1/2 × 2-1/2 × 14-1/4
B	Front	1/2 × 1-1/4 × 19-3/4
C	Bottom	1/4 × 13-5/8 × 19-1/8 plywood
D	Back	1/2 × 2-1/2 × 19-3/4
	Wood glue	

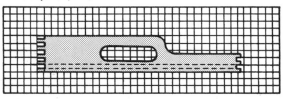

ONE SQUARE = 1/2"

SIDE PATTERN

COASTERS

1. Cut the parts to size using the dimensions given, then sand smooth. Cut the coasters (A) so that the grain runs diagonally to all four edges.
2. Shape the edges of the base (B) using a hand-held router equipped with a roman ogee bit.
3. Use a 1/4"-inch dado head set to a depth of 9/32" to cut the grooves in the coasters. Cut grooves 1/4" apart on one side of each piece, flip the piece over, rotate it 90°, and cut a second set of grooves.
4. Drill 1/4"-diameter holes 1/4" deep in the base to accommodate the dowels (C).
5. Glue the holders in place and check for squareness. Finish as desired.
6. Finish the coasters and holder as desired.

LIST OF MATERIALS (Coasters)

(finished dimensions in inches)

A	Coasters (4)	1/2 × 3-1/4 × 3-1/4
B	Base	1/2 × 4-1/4 × 4-1/4
C	Dowels (2)	1/4-dia. × 2-1/4
	Wood glue	

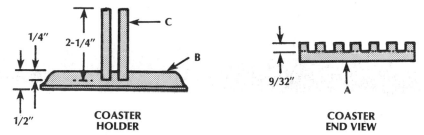

1/4"

2-1/4"

C

B

1/2"

COASTER HOLDER

9/32"

A

COASTER END VIEW

Toys and Games

A wooden toy is one of the most rewarding wood-working projects you can build. There are toys and games in this section suitable for children of all ages. They're also easy to build and tested for safety.

The game of Kalaha originated in Africa some seven thousand years ago, and it's just as popular today. The name is derived from the Kalahari Desert in South Africa where the natives played the game by scooping out pits in the sand—the same pits or hollows cut into the board shown here.

Here's everything you'll need to make the game, along with the rules of play.

1. Mark the fixture pattern on 3/8"-thick plywood; this will be the fixture template. Use a hole saw or jigsaw to cut out the template, then sand the edges to the pattern lines with a drum sander.

2. Screw the template to the unlaminated side of an 8" × 19" piece of prelaminated countertop material, which will serve as the fixture base (A).

3. Rout the template pattern 3/8" deep into the laminated side of the base using a pin router setup. This consists of a 3/4"-diameter pin mounted in the tabletop and a router mounted directly overhead. The template fits over the pin and the router is lowered into the work. As the work is moved around, the shape of the template is duplicated by the router cutting overhead. For these cuts use a 1/4"-diameter straight bit and a table pin of the same diameter.

4. Cut the fixture frame rails (B, C) and clamping block (D), preferably out of a hardwood such as maple. Bore two 7/8"-diameter holes 1/8" deep into the upper half of the inner face on one end piece. Then drill a 5/16"-diameter hole completely through each of the original holes for mounting tee nuts and thumbscrews, as shown in the drawing.

5. Turn the base over so its pattern side is down, then fasten the end rails to its ends using #10 wood screws. Make sure the rail with the thumbscrews is placed on the end of the base with the extra inch of space between it and the circles.

MAKING A GAME BOARD

1. To make a game board (E), cut a choice piece of 3/4" hardwood to 8" × 18". Set the piece into the fixture and push it flush against the end without the thumbscrews. Fit the clamping block against its other end and tighten the thumbscrews against it to hold the board firmly in place.

2. Fit a 1/2"-diameter carbide-tipped straight bit into the router and a 1"-diameter pin in the tabletop. Position the fixture over the pin and set the depth stop on the router so the cuts will go only 1/4" deep. Rout out the twelve circles and two hollows.

3. Switch to a 1/2"-diameter carbide-tipped core box router bit and a 1/2"-diameter table pin. Set the depth stop again to limit the plunge cut to a 1/4" depth. Round the edges of all the circles and hollows.

4. Remove the board from the fixture and cut a decorative shape along its lower edges using a router bit equipped with a pilot.

5. Saw the board in half, sand, and finish with two coats of polyurethane. After the finish has dried, install a pair of hinges and a clasp.

6. Use marbles, stones, or buckshot for the playing pieces, or cut up 3/8"-diameter dowel into small pieces of equal size.

THE RULES OF KALAHA

Two players sit behind two ranks of six pits. Each pit contains three balls. The purpose of the game is to accumulate as many balls as possi-

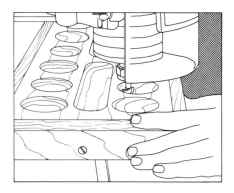

Using a core bit to round edges of the hollows.

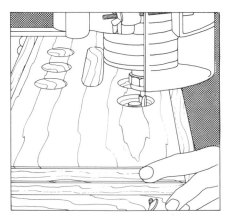

Routing out circles and hollows with an overarm router.

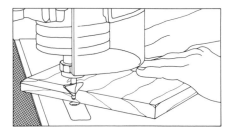

Cutting a decorative edge around the bottom of the board.

ble in the large bin (Kalaha) to each player's right.

Each player in turn picks up all the balls in any one of his own six pits and sows them, one in each pit, around the board to the right, including, if there are enough, his own Kalaha, and one into his opponent's pit (but not his Kalaha). If the player's last ball lands in his own Kalaha, he gets another turn. If it lands in an empty pit on his own side, he captures all his opponent's balls in the opposite pit and puts them in his own Kalaha together with the other captured balls.

The game is over when all six pits on one side (or the other) are empty. All balls in the pits on the opposite side go into the opponent's Kalaha and the score is determined by who has the most balls.

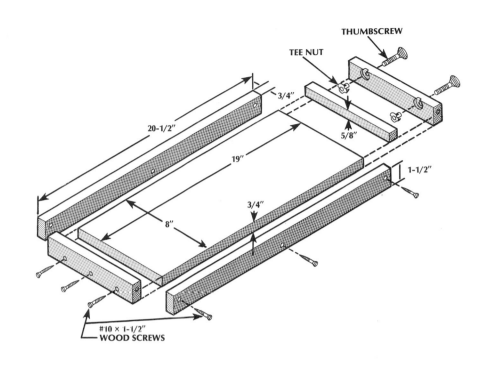

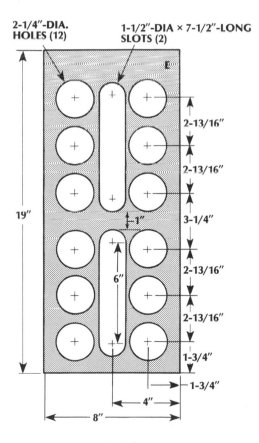

TEMPLATE DETAIL

LIST OF MATERIALS

(finished dimensions in inches)

A	Base	3/4 × 8 × 19
B	Side rails (2)	3/4 × 1-1/2 × 20-1/2
C	End rails (2)	3/4 × 1-1/2 × 8
D	Clamping block	3/4 × 5/8 × 8
E	Game board	3/4 × 8 × 18
	Flathead wood screws	#10 × 1-1/2
	Thumbscrews	
	Tee nuts	
	Hinges	
	Clasp	

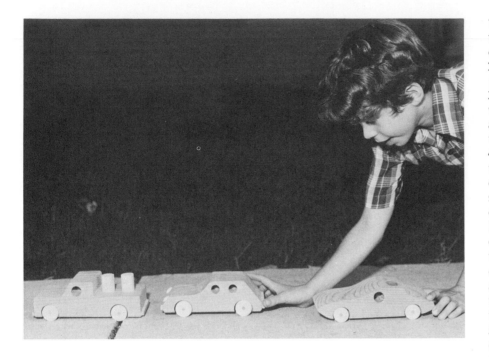

1. Make a cardboard template of the car design. Trace the pattern on a 4 × 4.
2. Cut the desired car body shape (A) with a bandsaw.
3. Drill the various holes for the windows, wheel wells, headlights, and axles. Use a Forstner bit to cut the wheel wells.
4. Using a hole saw, cut four wheels (B) to the dimensions given out of 3/4" scrap stock. The hole saw will simultaneously cut the outside contour and mark the axle hole of the wheel. Drill the 1/4"-diameter axle holes. As an alternative, the wheels can also be turned on your lathe. Drill a 1/4"-diameter axle hole through the middle of the block before turning, then turn the cylinder and cut it into wheels.
5. Before assembling the car, power sand and file each of the individual pieces.
6. Finish sand the pieces with a fine sandpaper (100 grit or finer).
7. To assemble the car, rub paraffin on the middle part of the axles (C) and slide them through the holes in the car body. Glue the wheels to the axle ends. Finally, glue the 1/2"-diameter dowel buttons into the headlight holes.
8. Check to make sure that the wheels and headlights cannot be removed by a child, then give the car a nontoxic finish.

In the future use these guidelines and your imagination to design vans, buses, taxis, fire engines, and other toy vehicles.

Remember how those toy cars you played with as a child never wore out? Now you can make those sturdy, all-wood toys again by following these simple plans. While specific features vary, each of these toy cars is made in the same fashion. Naturally, you might want to experiment with the designs to suit your own tastes.

LIST OF MATERIALS (Sedan)

(finished dimensions in inches)

A	Body	2-3/8 × 3-1/4 × 7-3/4
B	Wheels (4)	1/4 dia. × 3/4
C	Axles (2)	1/4 dia. × 3-1/4
D	Headlights (2)	1/2-dia. dowel buttons

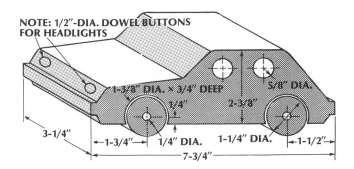

ONE SQUARE = 1/4"

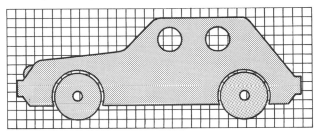

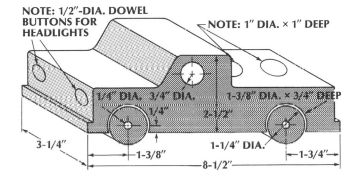

ONE SQUARE = 1/4"

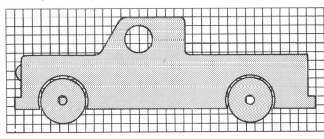

LIST OF MATERIALS (Pickup Truck)

(finished dimensions in inches)

A	Body	2-1/2 × 3-1/4 × 8-1/2
B	Wheels (4)	1-1/4 dia. × 3/4
C	Axles (2)	1/4 dia. × 3-1/4
D	Headlights (2)	1/2-dia. dowel buttons

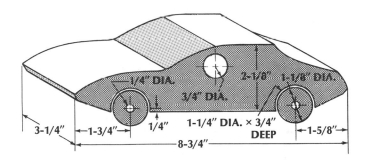

LIST OF MATERIALS (Sports Car)

(finished dimensions in inches)

A	Body	2-1/8 × 3-1/4 × 8-3/4
B	Wheels (4)	1-1/8 dia. × 3/4
C	Axles (2)	1/4 dia. × 3-1/4

ONE SQUARE = 1/4"

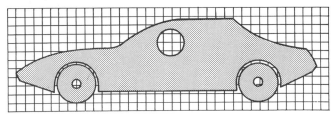

This sturdy tugboat floats on water, so a child can enjoy it in the bathtub or swimming pool. The all-wood design makes it safe to play with, and it can be built in no time at all. Be sure to use waterproof glue when assembling.

1. Cut blanks for the thicker pieces from 3/4″ stock face-laminated with water-resistant glue. Cut all pieces to the listed dimensions.

2. Cut out the shapes on a bandsaw using the patterns provided. When cutting the hull (A), set the bandsaw table at a 10° tilt; this will reduce the sanding needed to shape the contour.

3. Turn the smokestack (E) round on a lathe, then remove stock by sanding or rasping from both sides of the cylinder to make it oval-shaped. Angle the top of the smokestack and the deck house (C) at 10°.

4. Use a belt sander with a sanding drum to make the inside concave curves on the railing (B) and pilot house (D). Shape the hull with a convex curve as the sides taper in toward the keel, gradually at first and then sharply toward the bottom.

5. Rough sand all the pieces with coarse sandpaper, then repeat with gradually finer grits. If using a belt sander, always keep the workpiece moving to eliminate any large flat spots in the contour.

6. Before final assembly, test the tugboat to make sure it floats evenly. Attach the railing to the hull and carefully set them in the water. Move the pilot house, deck house, and smokestack into a position that enables the tugboat to float upright and level.

7. Mark the exact position of the parts, then assemble using waterproof glue and clamps. Dowels can also be used for added strength.

8. Finish as desired.

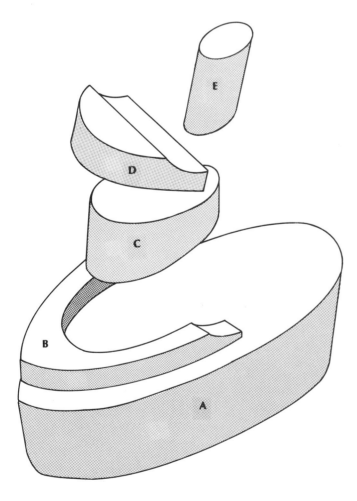

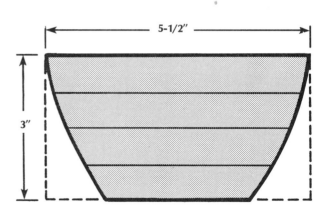

HULL FRONT VIEW

5-1/2″

3″

LIST OF MATERIALS

(finished dimensions in inches)

A	Hull	3 × 5-1/2 × 12
B	Railing	3/4 × 5-1/2 × 7
C	Deck house	2-1/4 × 3 × 5
D	Pilot house	1-1/2 × 4 × 3-1/4
E	Smokestack	1-1/2 × 1-1/2 × 4
	Water-resistant wood glue	

ONE SQUARE = 1/4″

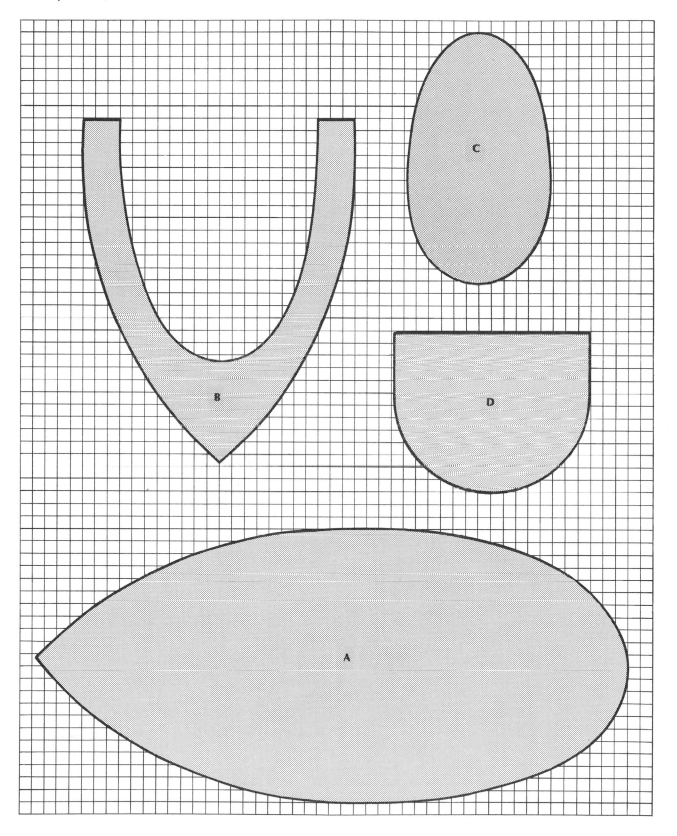

Puzzles have always fascinated children and adults alike. Here are five fun animal puzzles you can make on a bandsaw or jigsaw: a bear (A), owl (B), duck (C), elephant (D), and kangaroo (E).

1. Make two templates of each puzzle design—one template for the outside shape and one for the inside individual pieces. Use 1-1/2"-thick stock or two pieces of 3/4" stock face-laminated together, cutting the pieces 1/4" wider and 1/4" longer than the dimensions called for.

2. Trace the ouside and inside patterns on the workpieces. On a bandsaw or jigsaw, cut the outside shape first, then cut the individual pieces apart.

3. Using a disc sander or belt sander, sand all of the outside surfaces of the puzzle pieces.

4. If desired, use a nontoxic stain, such as food coloring, to highlight certain parts of the puzzles or to create contrasts between parts.

LIST OF MATERIALS

(finished dimensions in inches)

A	Bear	1-1/2 × 8-3/4 × 10-7/8
B	Owl	1-1/2 × 8-1/2 × 11-5/8
C	Duck	1-1/2 × 11-5/8 × 8-3/8
D	Elephant	1-1/2 × 12 × 8-3/8
E	Kangaroo	1-1/2 × 8-1/2 × 11-5/8

ONE SQUARE = 1/4"

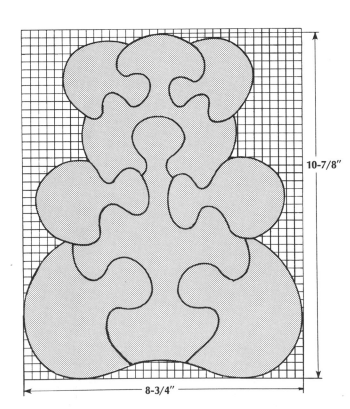

10-7/8"

8-3/4"

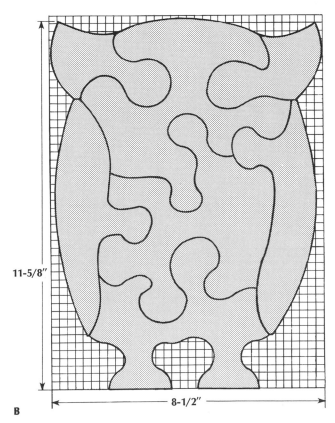

11-5/8"

8-1/2"

B

ONE SQUARE = 1/4"

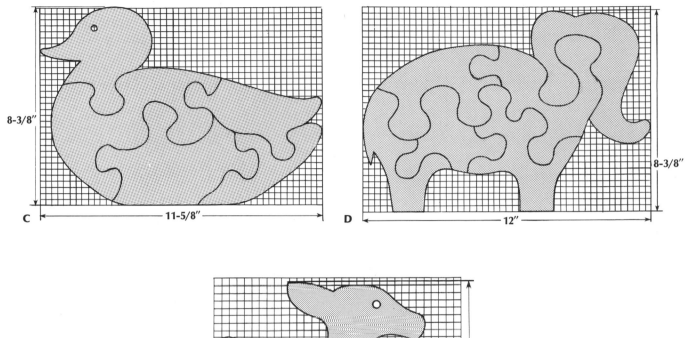

C   8-3/8"   11-5/8"

D   8-3/8"   12"

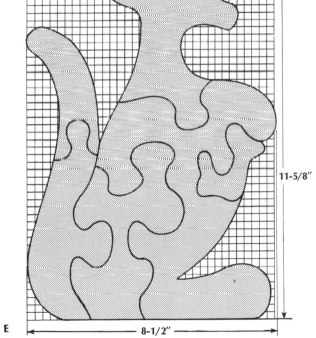

E   11-5/8"   8-1/2"

3. Glue and clamp the legs and crosspieces together.

4. Cut one end of each tray side (D) at a 10° angle; the other end is mitered 45° as shown. The tray fronts (C) are mitered 45° on each end.

5. Cut a groove 3/8" deep and 1/4" wide 3/8" above the bottom of the tray fronts and sides.

6. With the tray bottoms (E) in place, construct the trays using glue and 1-1/4" brads. Attach two glue blocks (F) to each tray with a slight setback to hold the trays snug when screwed to the frame.

7. Connect the two easel frames with a piano hinge and folding leg braces. Position the braces to allow the easel to open wide enough to prevent it from tipping over.

8. Fasten the faces (G) to the easel frames using glue and #8 flathead wood screws, making their top edges flush. Drill three evenly spaced 1/4"-diameter holes through each face and into the top crosspiece on each side. In each hole, glue a 1/4"-diameter dowel that has been tapered to a dull point.

9. Fasten the trays to the easel faces using glue and #10 flathead wood screws. Center the trays across the width of the faces and make their lower edges flush.

10. To complete the easel, fill all screw holes with putty, and finish as desired.

Here's a project guaranteed to provide hours of fun for your children: a lightweight, collapsible easel with a dent-free surface made from 1/4" hardboard.

1. Cut all of the pieces to size according to the dimensions provided. Cut a dado 3/8" deep and 2-1/2" wide approximately 12-1/2" from the bottom of each leg (A).

2. Rabbet the ends of the crosspieces (B) and the tops of the legs to the same dimensions as the dado cuts made in the previous step.

LIST OF MATERIALS

(finished dimensions in inches)

A	Legs (4)	3/4 × 2-1/2 × 60
B	Crosspieces (4)	3/4 × 2-1/2 × 30
C	Tray fronts (2)	3/4 × 2-1/2 × 22
D	Tray sides (4)	3/4 × 2-1/2 × 5
E	Tray bottoms (2)	1/4 × 4-1/2 × 21-1/4
F	Glue blocks (4)	3/4 × 3/4 × 2
G	Faces (2)	1/4 × 30 × 47-1/2
	Flathead wood screws	#8 × 1
	Flathead wood screws	#10 × 1-1/4
	Dowels	1/4 dia. × 2-1/2
	Brads	
	Piano hinge	
	Folding leg braces (2)	
	Wood glue	

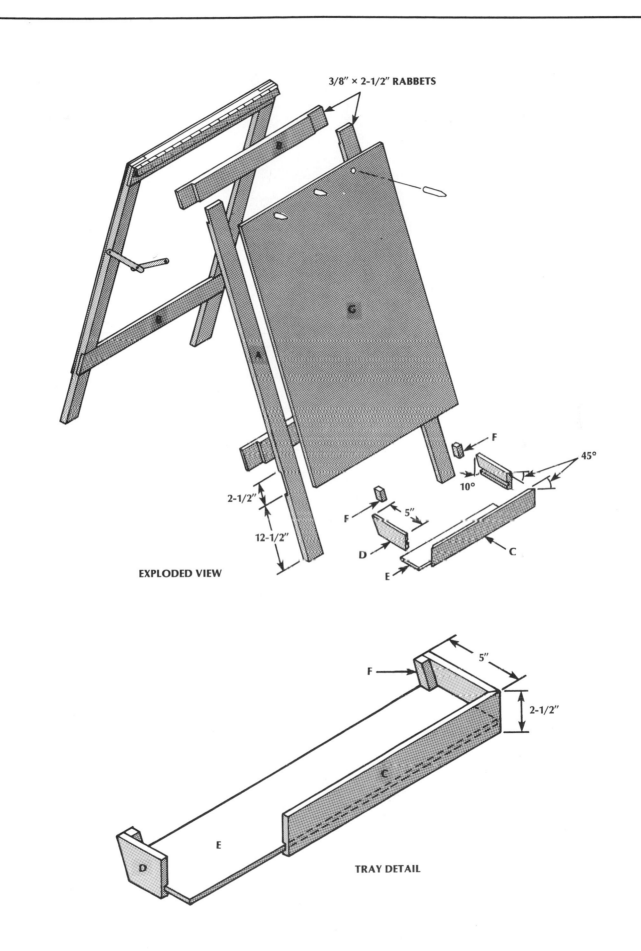

3/8″ × 2-1/2″ RABBETS

EXPLODED VIEW

2-1/2″

12-1/2″

F

F

5″

D

E

C

45°

10°

TRAY DETAIL

F

5″

2-1/2″

D

E

C

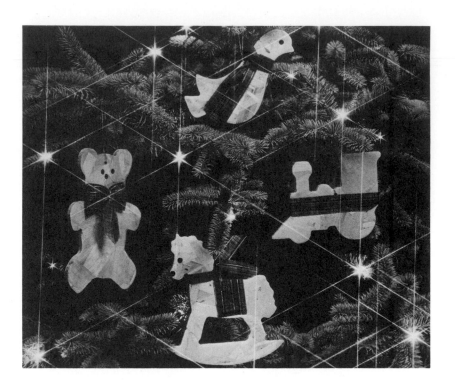

Nothing adds to the beauty and wonder of the family Christmas tree quite like homemade ornaments. These eye-catching figurines can be made easily from 1/2" wood on a bandsaw or jigsaw. Your children are sure to want them all: the bear (A), dove (B), hobbyhorse (C), and train (D).

1. Make a template of the figurines using the patterns provided.

2. Cut out the shapes on a bandsaw or jigsaw, then use a disc sander or belt sander to sand all of the outside surfaces.

3. Finish the figurines as desired, or leave them unfinished for a more rustic look. Add ribbon as shown for a final touch.

LIST OF MATERIALS

(finished dimensions in inches)

A	Bear	1/2 × 3-1/4 × 4-1/2
B	Dove	1/2 × 3-1/8 × 3-1/8
C	Hobbyhorse	1/2 × 3-1/2 × 3-7/8
D	Train	1/2 × 2-5/8 × 3-1/2

ONE SQUARE = 3/16"

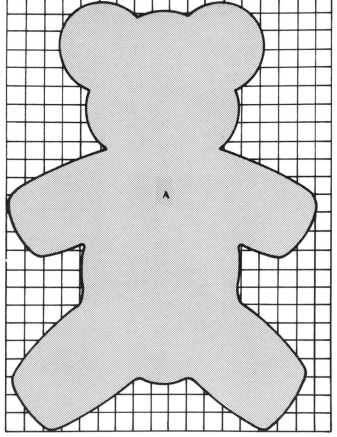

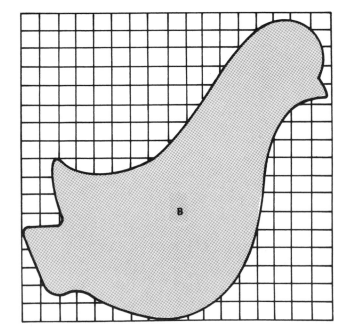

ONE SQUARE = 3/16″

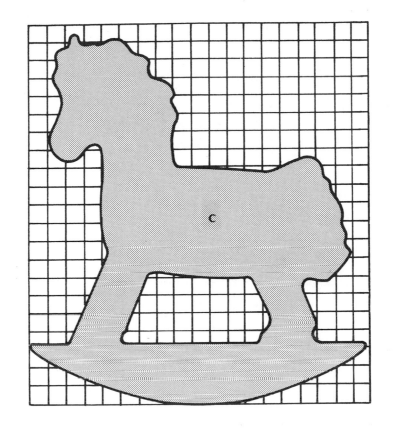

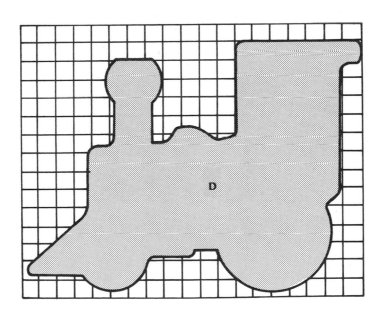

plate out of cardboard. With careful arrangement you should be able to lay out all four legs on an 18" length of 5/4 × 12 stock. Cut out the legs with a bandsaw or saber saw.

NOTE: The edge of the notch at the bottom of each leg must be angled 12° off square so that all four legs will slope in toward the horse's middle. If you prefer, cut out the legs without notches first, then figure out the notches during assembly. The length of the notches is not critical, so long as they are the same on all four legs and the tips of the legs remain above the bottom of the runners after assembly.

4. Lay out the two runners (D) on one side of a 31" length of 5/4 × 12 stock. Set them closely together so that enough width remains on the board for cutting out the seat. Use a bandsaw or saber saw to cut out the runners.

5. Lay out the seat (B) on one end of the board from which the runners were taken. Cut out the seat

A rocking horse is one of those toys that never goes out of style. The one shown here is designed for sturdiness as well as stability. The runners are spread far enough apart to prevent a small child from tipping over, and the tail is left mostly connected with the body so it cannot easily be broken off. The horse shown in the photo was made from 5/4 Philippine mahogany stepping material, except for the handle, which was formed from a hardwood dowel. Substitute other woods if you like, but always use quality material for a toy that can be passed along in your family for generations to come.

1. Use the pattern provided to make a template for cutting out the horse's body (A). Tape or glue the pattern to a 23" length of 5/4 × 12 stock, then cut out the profile with a bandsaw or saber saw.

2. While the pattern is still attached to the body, bore a starter hole for the teardrop opening in the tail area, then use a saber saw to complete the cut. Also, mark and drill a 1/2"-diameter hole through the head for inserting the handle (F) and two pairs of holes of the same

size in the areas where you want to attach the legs (C).

3. Since exact duplicates are needed for the four legs, it is a good idea to make the leg tem-

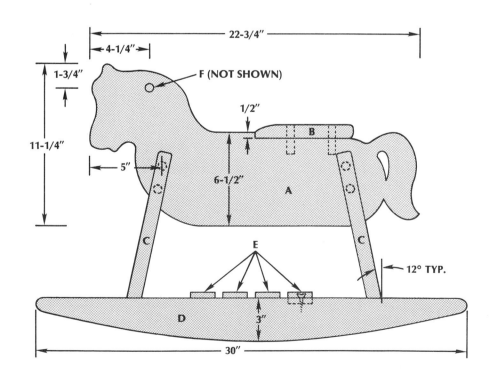

with a bandsaw or saber saw, then use a drawknife or other appropriate tool to slope its front so that it ends up only about 9/16" thick at the point where it will join the middle of the horse's back.

6. Rip and crosscut the remainder of the 31"-long board into the four runner spacer slats (E). Then sand all the pieces cut thus far and round over their sharp edges.

7. Begin the assembly by drilling holes in the legs for fastening them to the body. Hold a leg in place and drill through the holes already in the body into that leg. Then remove the leg and repeat the procedure with the leg that fits on the opposite side of the horse.

8. Once all four legs are properly drilled, fasten them to the horse using glue and 1/2"-diameter dowels. Be sure to check the relationship of the dowel length and hole depths before gluing.

9. Once the legs are in place, fit the runners beneath them. Fasten the legs to the runners using glue and #8 × 1-1/4" flathead wood screws. Counterbore the screws.

10. Measure the distance between runners, then rabbet the ends of all the runner spacer slats so that they fit snugly into that space. The depth of the rabbets is a matter of taste; just make sure all are cut the same. Center the entire group of slats between the legs and space them about 1/2" apart.

11. Fasten the slats to the runners using glue and #8 × 1-1/4" flathead wood screws. Counterbore the screws slightly below the surface.

12. Lay out and drill parallel 1/2"-diameter holes in the seat and in the horse's back. Fasten the seat in place using glue and 1/2"-diameter dowels.

13. Cut a piece of 1/2"-diameter dowel 7" in length and run it through the hole in the horse's head. Center the dowel, then secure it in place by driving a screw down through the head into the dowel. Use a wood rasp and sandpaper to shape the dowel into a form comfortable for small hands.

14. If you wish, fill the counterbored screw holes with wood plugs or putty. Give the horse a final touchup sanding and apply the nontoxic finish of your choice.

ONE SQUARE = 1/2"

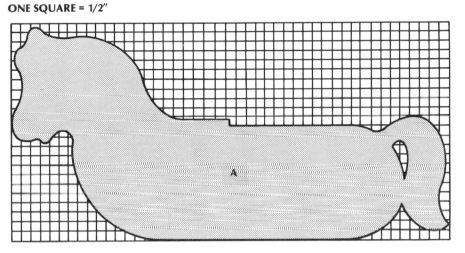

BODY CUTTING DETAIL

LIST OF MATERIALS

(finished dimensions in inches)

A	Body	1-1/8 × 11-1/4 × 22-3/4
B	Seat	1-1/8 × 5 × 6-7/8
C	Legs (4)	1-1/8 × 3-1/2 × 12-3/4
D	Runners (2)	1-1/8 × 3 × 30
E	Spacer slats (4)	1-1/8 × 1-3/4 × 12
F	Handle	1/2 dia. × 7
	Dowels (4)	1/2 dia. × 5
	Flathead wood screws	#8 × 1-1/4
	Wood glue	

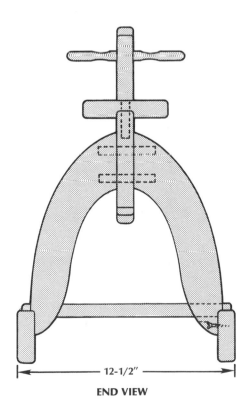

← 12-1/2" →

END VIEW

ONE SQUARE = 1/2"

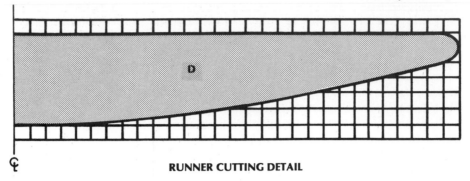

RUNNER CUTTING DETAIL

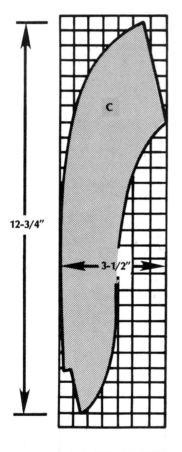

12-3/4"

3-1/2"

LEG CUTTING DETAIL

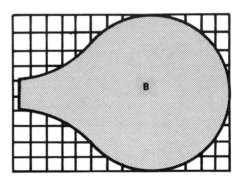

SEAT CUTTING DETAIL

ONE SQUARE = 1/2"

Here's a toy that's sure to fascinate children: a duck that waddles across tabletops. It's powered by a 5/8" steel hex nut that acts as a drive weight. Just hang the hex nut over the edge of a table and give the duck a nudge sideways; it will rock from side to side and walk toward the edge of the table.

1. Make full-size templates for the body (A) and legs (B) using the patterns provided. Cut out the shapes and rout or sand all edges.

2. Drill a 1/4"-diameter eye hole and a 1/4"-diameter hole to accommodate the leg pivot (C) in the body where indicated.

3. After cutting the leg pivot to size, drill a 3/32"-diameter hole 3/16" in from each end to accept the drawstrings.

4. Glue the leg pivot in place in the body.

5. Drill a 9/32"-diameter hole in each leg where indicated to accept the leg pivot.

6. Sand the bottom edge of each leg so that it angles 10° up toward the outside.

7. Slide two flat washers and one leg onto each side of the leg pivot.

8. Tie a drawstring to each end of the leg pivot, and tie the free ends of both drawstrings to the hex nut.

9. Finish as desired, and the duck will be ready to waddle.

LIST OF MATERIALS

(finished dimensions in inches)

A	Body	3/4 × 5 × 8-1/2
B	Legs (2)	1-1/8 × 4-3/4 × 5
C	Leg pivot	1/4 dia. × 4
	Flat washers (4)	
	Drawstring	#18 nylon cord
	Steel hex nut	5/8
	Wood glue	

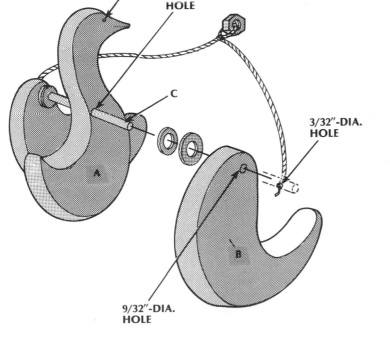

EYE HOLE

1/4"-DIA. HOLE

C

3/32"-DIA. HOLE

A

B

9/32"-DIA. HOLE

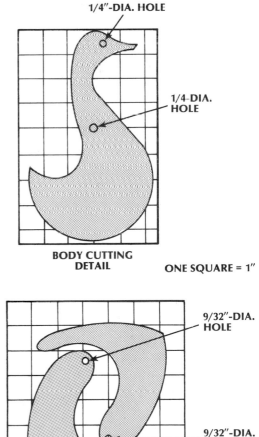

1/4"-DIA. HOLE

1/4-DIA. HOLE

BODY CUTTING DETAIL

ONE SQUARE = 1"

9/32"-DIA. HOLE

9/32"-DIA. HOLE

LEG CUTTING DETAIL

Indoor Projects

This section provides an interesting mix of indoor projects. Although most of them require more time and work to complete than the preceding projects, we think you'll agree that they are well worth the effort. And not only will you gain a sense of accomplishment after completing them but you'll also end up with very practical, beautiful pieces.

The butcher block has fallen out of favor in recent years, replaced by the countertop cutting board in an attempt to save space. This design, however, makes the butcher block a useful part of the kitchen once again. It has a drawer and shelves for storage, it can be moved to provide a cutting surface or extra counter space wherever needed, and it even has space for a microwave oven. In addition to the stand, plans are included for building a storage unit on the lower shelf in place of the oven.

MAKING THE STAND

1. Cut all pieces to size according to the dimensions given.

2. If you want to make the stand mobile and add casters to the legs (A), cut 2" off the length of the legs and drill a center hole in the bottom of each one to accept the caster shaft.

3. Lay out the positions of the rail joints on the legs as indicated in the drawings. Note that all rails are centered on the width of the legs and that the tops of the upper rails (B, E) and legs are flush. The lower rails (C, F) should be set 14-3/4"

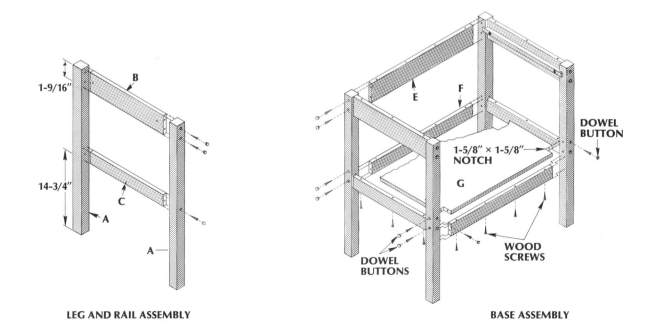

LEG AND RAIL ASSEMBLY

BASE ASSEMBLY

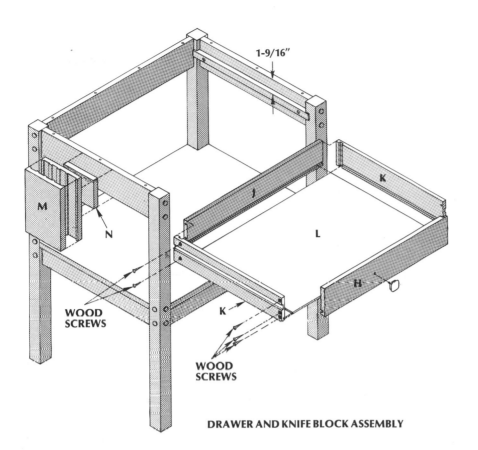

1-9/16"

WOOD SCREWS

M

N

K

WOOD SCREWS

DRAWER AND KNIFE BLOCK ASSEMBLY

1-5/8" × 1-5/8" notches on each corner of the shelf for fitting it between the legs.

7. Fasten the legs and rails together using wood glue and #8 × 1-3/4" wood screws. Then fasten the shelf in place, running #8 × 1-3/4" screws through the rails into its underside.

8. Position the drawer guides against the inside faces and 1-9/16" below the upper edges of the upper end rails. Fasten the guides to the rails using wood glue and #6 × 1-1/4" wood screws. Countersink the screws so their heads will not interfere with the operation of the drawers.

9. Cut a 3/4"-wide × 1/4"-deep groove 1" below the upper edge along the outside face of each drawer side (K). Check the fit between these grooves and the drawer guides. If necessary, widen the grooves to allow the drawer sides to slide smoothly back and forth on the guides.

10. Cut 1/2"-wide × 1/2"-deep rabbets across the ends of the drawer

above the bottoms of the legs, unless the shelf (G) will house a microwave oven. In that case, drop the lower rails 4".

4. Drill, countersink, and counterbore pilot holes for a pair of #8 wood screws at each joint between rails and legs. Drill through the legs into the ends of the rails and make the counterbores 3/8" in diameter and 3/4" deep.

5. Drill another set of counterbored pilot holes for #8 screws through each of the lower rails—three holes in each end rail and four in each front and back rail. Run the holes through the width of the rails, from the lower to the upper edges, and make the counterbores 1-3/8" deep. It might help to drill the counterbores first, then use a long, thin bit to complete the pilot holes.

6. Cut 3/8"-wide × 1/2"-deep rabbets across the rear ends and 1" × 1/2" rabbets across the front ends of the drawer guides (D). Also, cut

LIST OF MATERIALS (Stand)

(finished dimensions in inches)

A	Legs (4)	1-3/4 × 1-3/4 × 34
B	Upper end rails (2)	3/4 × 4 × 18-3/4
C	Lower end rails (2)	3/4 × 2-1/2 × 18-3/4
D	Drawer guides (2)	3/4 × 3/4 × 20-1/8
E	Upper back rail (2)	3/4 × 4 × 24-3/4
F	Lower back and front rails (2)	3/4 × 2-1/2 × 24-3/4
G	Shelf	3/4 × 22 × 28
H	Drawer front	3/4 × 4 × 24-5/8
J	Drawer back	1/2 × 3-1/2 × 24-1/8
K	Drawer sides (2)	1/2 × 3-1/2 × 18
L	Drawer bottom	1/4 × 17-1/2 × 24-1/8 plywood
M	Knife block (2)	3/4 × 6 × 9
N	Spacer block	5/8 × 5 × 4
P	Butcher block top pieces (28)	3/4 × 2 × 28-1/2
Q	Top facings (2)	3/4 × 2 × 32-1/2
R	Handle	1 dia. × 22-1/2
	Threaded metal rods (4)	3/8 dia. × 20-7/8
	Flathead wood screws	#6 × 1-1/4
	Flathead wood screws	#8 × 1-1/2
	Flathead wood screws	#8 × 1-3/4
	Washers and nuts	
	Dowel buttons and dowel plugs	3/8 dia.
	Drawer pull	
	Wood glue	

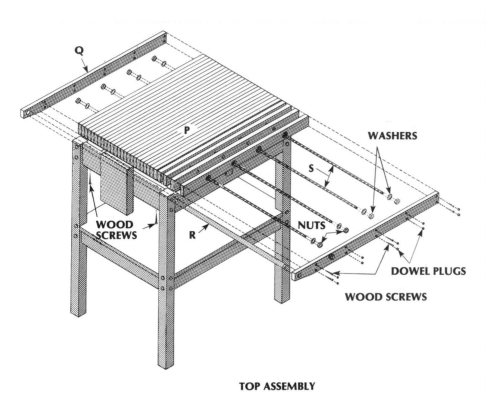

TOP ASSEMBLY

front (H) to receive the ends of the sides. Cut 1/4"-deep × 1/2"-wide dadoes across the drawer sides, 1/2" in from the rear, to receive the ends of the back (J). Cut 1/4"-deep × 1/4"-wide grooves in the drawer front, back, and sides, 1/4" above their lower edges, to receive the bottom (L).

11. Center and drill a screw hole through the drawer front for attaching the pull. Countersink screw holes through the drawer sides where they will attach to the ends of the front and back. Then assemble the drawer. Use glue and #6 × 1-1/4" flathead wood screws to join the sides, front, and back, but leave the bottom unglued in the grooves.

12. Drill four evenly spaced 3/8"-diameter holes through each butcher block top piece (P) to receive the metal reinforcing rods. Counterbore the holes in the outer two pieces to make room for the nuts and washers.

13. Spread waterproof glue between all adjacent butcher block top pieces. Thread the rods through

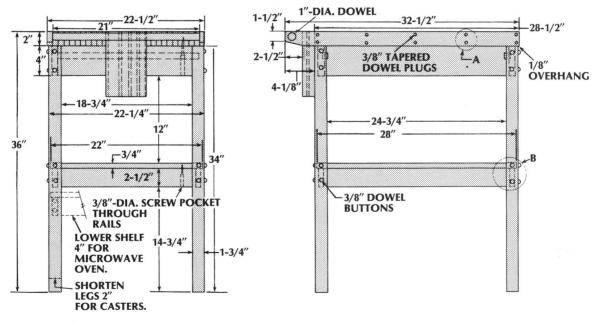

BUTCHER BLOCK MICROWAVE STAND LAYOUT

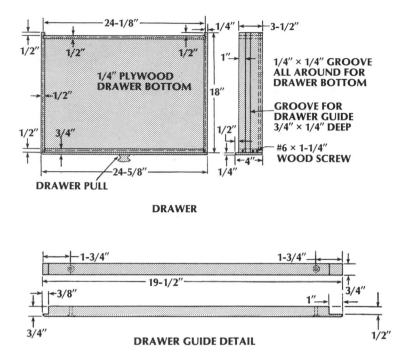

DRAWER

1/4" × 1/4" GROOVE ALL AROUND FOR DRAWER BOTTOM

GROOVE FOR DRAWER GUIDE 3/4" × 1/4" DEEP

#6 × 1-1/4" WOOD SCREW

DRAWER PULL

DRAWER GUIDE DETAIL

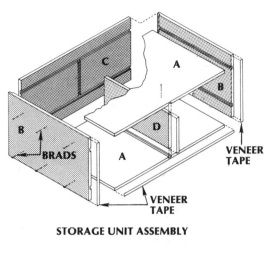

STORAGE UNIT ASSEMBLY

the pieces and install the nuts and washers. Tighten the nuts to align and clamp the pieces while the glue dries.

14. Trim one end of each facing (Q) to the profile shown in the stand layout drawing and drill holes for the ends of the handle (R). Begin the tapers 3" from the ends and center the holes 1-1/4" from the ends of the facing pieces.

15. Fasten the facings to the top using waterproof glue and #8 × 1-1/2" flathead wood screws, making their right ends and upper edges flush. Glue the handle in place at the same time. Position the screw holes where you will not hit the metal rods. Counterbore the holes and fill them with 3/8"-diameter plugs.

16. Sand the top and facings flush, then finish them with mineral oil or a similar nontoxic finish. Sand the rest of the stand, fill the counterbored holes with wood buttons, then apply polyurethane or another finish of choice.

17. Center the top on the frame and mark the position of the screw holes in the upper edges of the rails. Drill pilot holes into the un-

derside of the block top, then fasten it to the rails using #8 × 1-3/4" flathead wood screws.

18. Cut matching 1/16"-deep grooves in the two halves of the knife block (M). Then glue the pieces together, aligning the grooves. Nail or screw the 5/8"-thick spacer block (N) to the left end rail, then glue the knife block to the spacer, making its top flush with the upper surface of the butcher block.

MAKING THE STORAGE UNIT

1. Cut all pieces to size from 1/2"-thick veneer plywood.

LIST OF MATERIALS (Storage Unit)

(finished dimensions in inches)

A	Top and bottom (2)	1/2 × 16-3/4 × 24 plywood
B	Sides (2)	1/2 × 11-1/2 × 17 plywood
C	Back	1/2 × 11-1/2 × 24 plywood
D	Divider	1/2 × 7 × 16-3/4 plywood
	Wire brads	#17 × 1
	Veneer tape	
	Wood filler	
	Wood glue	

2. Cut 1/2"-wide × 1/4"-deep rabbets across the rear ends of the sides (B) and 1/2" × 1/4" grooves, spaced 6-1/2" apart, along the length of the sides and back (C). Also, cut 1/2" × 1/4" dadoes across the center of the top and bottom (A) and back. The dado on the back should only connect the two grooves.

3. Assemble the unit with glue and #17 × 1" wire brads. Set the brads and fill with a wood filler that matches the finish you will be using.

4. Cover all exposed edges of the plywood with veneer tape.

5. Finish the drawer to match the stand and storage unit, then install.

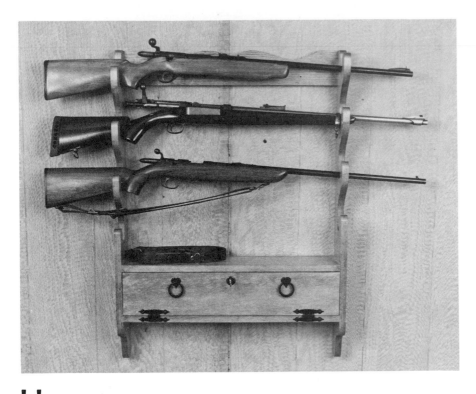

Here's the ideal method of storing those prized rifles and fishing rods—the sportsman's rack. Not only does it make an eye-catching display, but it also has a locking compartment for storing shells, lures, and other items.

1. Select two 8' lengths of good quality 1 × 6 lumber, hardwood or softwood. Cut the top (A), sides (B), shelves (C), and door (E) to length, then rip them to width. Rip the pieces 1/16" wide at first, then use a jointer or hand plane to clean up the ripped edges.

2. Cut a pair of 1/2"-wide × 1/4"-deep dadoes across the inner face of each side piece to receive the ends of the shelves. Space the dadoes 5" apart and set the lower one 5-1/2" above the bottom end of each board, as shown in the front view drawing.

3. Cut a 1/4"-wide × 1/4"-deep rabbet along the back edge of each side piece in the area between the dadoes to make room for the ends of the plywood back panel.

4. Cut 1/4"-wide × 1/4"-deep rabbets along what will become the inside rear edges of the shelves to accept the upper and lower edges of the back panel.

5. Cut a 4"-long notch 3/4" deep into the rear edge at the upper end of each side piece to make room for the ends of the rack's top rail (A).

6. Dry assemble the pieces to make sure everything fits correctly. Fine tune the joinery as needed.

7. Begin the layout of the curved shapes on the top rail and side pieces by making templates from cardboard or heavy paper using the patterns provided as guides. Then use the templates to trace the patterns onto the boards.

8. Before laying out the hook patterns on the side pieces, decide how you want to use the rack. If you want it to serve as a gun rack, set the hooks on the left side 1-1/2" lower than those on the right, as shown in the front view drawing. But, if you want the rack to hold fishing gear, lay out the hook patterns the same way on both side pieces.

9. Use a bandsaw or saber saw to cut out the patterns traced on the top rail and sides. Make relief cuts into the hook pockets before cutting around the tight inside corners. Cut along the outside of the lines, then smooth the edges while sanding down to the lines.

10. Center the latch plate part of the lock next to the front edge on the underside of the top shelf. Mark around it, then chisel out the shelf as needed for mounting the plate.

11. Clamp the top rail, sides, and shelves together while drilling pilot holes for #8 wood screws. Drill 3/8"-diameter × 1/4"-deep counterbore holes over the pilot holes in the sides and countersink the holes that run through the back of the top rail.

LIST OF MATERIALS

(finished dimensions in inches)

A	Top	3/4 × 4 × 26
B	Sides (2)	3/4 × 5 × 36
C	Shelves (2)	3/4 × 5 × 25
D	Back	1/4 × 5-1/2 × 25
E	Door	3/4 × 4-15/16 × 24-7/16
	Dowel buttons or plugs	3/8 dia. × 1/4
	Flathead wood screws	#8 × 1-1/4
	Wire nails	
	Hinges with screws (2 sets)	
	Magnetic catch and plate	
	Lock and key	
	Door pulls	
	Hanging hardware	
	Wood glue	

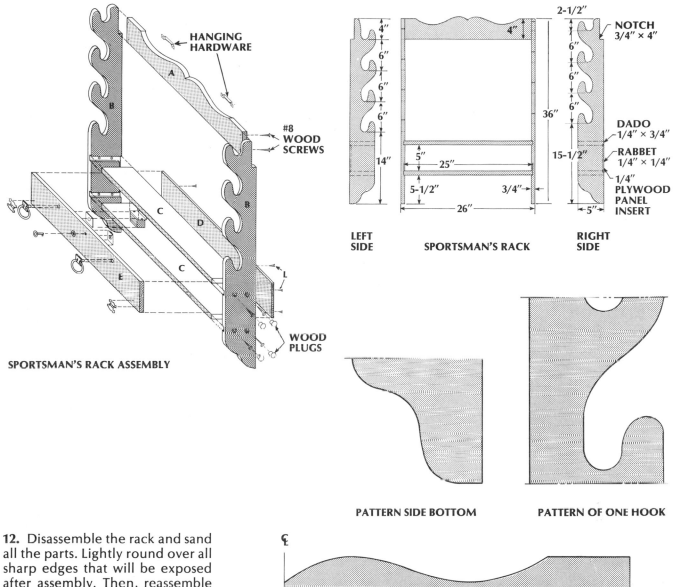

HANGING HARDWARE

#8 WOOD SCREWS

A

B

B

C

D

C

E

L

WOOD PLUGS

SPORTSMAN'S RACK ASSEMBLY

2-1/2"

4"

4"

6"

6"

6"

6"

NOTCH 3/4" × 4"

6"

6"

6"

36"

DADO 1/4" × 3/4"

14"

5"

25"

15-1/2"

RABBET 1/4" × 1/4"

5-1/2"

3/4"

1/4" PLYWOOD PANEL INSERT

26"

5"

LEFT SIDE

SPORTSMAN'S RACK

RIGHT SIDE

PATTERN SIDE BOTTOM

PATTERN OF ONE HOOK

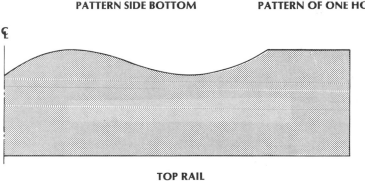

TOP RAIL

12. Disassemble the rack and sand all the parts. Lightly round over all sharp edges that will be exposed after assembly. Then, reassemble the shelves, sides, and top rail using wood glue and #8 × 1-1/4" flathead wood screws.

13. Cut a piece of 1/4" plywood to size for the back (D). Fasten the back to the shelves and sides using glue and wire nails.

14. Glue 3/8"-diameter wood plugs in the counterbored screw holes. After the glue dries, sand the plugs flush with the sides.

15. Temporarily mount the hinges on the door, then fit the door in place and fasten the hinges to the bottom shelf. Check to see that the door operates properly, then mark the location for the lock keyhole.

16. Remove the hinges from the door and shelf. Drill the keyhole in the door, as well as holes for the door pulls.

17. Sand the door, breaking all sharp edges. Apply the desired finish to the door and the rest of the rack. After the finish has dried, mount all the hardware on the door and rack, including your choice of hardware for hanging the rack on the wall.

How many times have you stretched out on your favorite easy chair, only to realize that the book or magazine you wanted to read is on the other side of the room? With this attractive chairside bookcase, reading material is always within reach. In addition, the top shelf can be used to display knick-knacks, small plants, or even a reading lamp.

1. To begin, cut the pieces to size according to the dimensions given.

2. Drill 3/8"-diameter dowel holes 1-1/16" deep in the ends and sides of the end rails (A). Using dowel centers, transfer the centers of the holes to the stiles (B). Be sure to mark the centers accurately to ensure proper assembly.

3. Assemble the end rails, rods (E) and rails with dowels by gluing and clamping in place. Allow the glue sufficient time to dry before continuing.

4. Drill pilot holes in the rails and shelves (C) for the bracket screws, and attach the brackets to the stiles.

5. Attach the shelf backs (D) to the stiles with 6d finishing nails.

6. To complete the assembly, attach the shelves to the brackets with screws.

7. Sand with 150-grit paper, followed by 180-grit. Finish as desired.

LIST OF MATERIALS

(finished dimensions in inches)

A	End rails (6)	3/4 × 4 × 5
B	Stiles (4)	3/4 × 2-1/2 × 32-1/2
C	Shelves (3)	3/4 × 9 × 25-1/2
D	Shelf backs (3)	3/4 × 4 × 25-1/2
E	Rods (8)	3/8 dia. × 10-3/4
	Dowels	3/8 dia. × 2
	Metal shelf brackets (12)	3/8 × 1-1/2 × 1-1/2
	6d finishing nails	
	Wood glue	

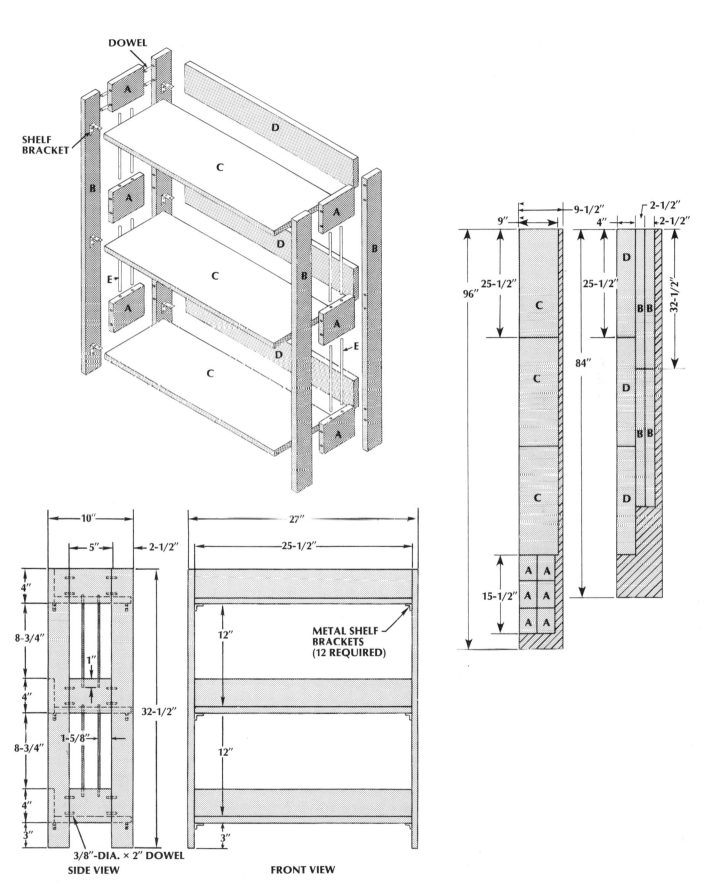

DOWEL

SHELF
BRACKET

A

D

C

A

A

D

C

B

E

A

D

C

B

A

E

A

A

B

D

C

C

C

9"
9-1/2"
2-1/2"
4"
2-1/2"
2-1/2"

96"
25-1/2"
D
25-1/2"
32-1/2"

84"
D

B B

D

B B

D

A A

15-1/2"
A A
A A

10"
5"
2-1/2"

4"

8-3/4"

1"

4"

1-5/8"
32-1/2"

8-3/4"

4"

3"

3/8"-DIA. × 2" DOWEL
SIDE VIEW

27"
25-1/2"

12"
METAL SHELF
BRACKETS
(12 REQUIRED)

12"

3"
FRONT VIEW

It's becoming more and more expensive these days to own good handcrafted furniture. This project enables you to make your own armchair at a fraction of the retail cost. What's more, you'll be sure of the craftsmanship and quality, because you made it yourself.

1. Cut the pieces to size according to the dimensions given. When ripping the back cleat (L) to width, cut a 16° bevel on the ripped edge. Also, cut tapers on the ends of the back supports (K) as shown.

2. Drill 1-3/8"-deep × 1"-wide × 2-1/4"-long mortises in the arms (A) and legs (B) as shown. Remove any excess stock with a hand chisel.

3. Use a router or hand chisel to make the 1/2"-deep × 3/8"-wide × 2-1/2"-long mortises in the edges of the back rails (G, H). Leave the corners round.

4. Mark the locations for cutting tenons in the ends of the side rails (C), front rail (E), and back rails. To mark, score the wood with a knife to prevent splintering.

5. Use a dado blade to cut the 1"-thick × 2-1/4"-wide × 1-1/4"-long tenons.

6. Drill dowel holes in the arms, side rails, side panels (D), and back stiles (F), and rails. Drill these holes 1" deep.

7. Round the side edges of the slats (J) with a router and rounding over bit. This will enable them to fit the mortises in the back rails.

8. Sand all pieces smooth with 150-grit paper. Dry-assemble the armchair to check for fit.

9. Assemble the side frames. Begin by fitting the side rails between the legs, then install the side panels and the arms. Use glue in all joints and clamp until dry.

10. Fit the slats between the top and bottom back rails. Fasten the rails to the stiles using glue and dowels. Clamp and set aside for the glue to dry.

11. Assemble the front rail and the side frames using glue in the mortise and tenon joints. Clamp the assembly, then immediately install the front (M) and side (N) cleats. Butt the side cleats against the back of the front rail and set them 1/16" to 1/8" below the upper edges of the side rails. Drill pilot holes counterbored at least 1/4" deep, then fasten the cleats to the frames using glue and #10 × 2-1/4" flathead wood screws. If you prefer, dry assemble the frames and rail while drilling pilot holes in the cleats and frames, then remove the front rail while you install the side cleats. Glue the front rail in place after that.

12. Fit the back cleat in place against the tail ends of the side cleats, making their upper edges flush. Fasten the back cleat to the side cleats using #10 × 2-1/4" flathead wood screws set in pilot holes counterbored to a depth of at least 1/2".

13. Hold the back frame in position between the sides with its lower rail pressed firmly against the back cleat. Mark the side frames along the rear edge of the back. Remove the back frame and install the back supports using glue and #8 × 1-1/4" flathead wood screws, countersunk or slightly counterbored. Then fasten the back frame in place by running screws through its bottom rail into the back cleat and through the supports into its stiles.

14. Do all final sanding, then finish the chair frame as desired.

15. When the finish has dried, mount band irons to the cleats with

LIST OF MATERIALS

(finished dimensions in inches)

A	Arms (2)	1-1/2 × 3-1/4 × 26-1/2
B	Legs (4)	1-1/2 × 3-1/4 × 24
C	Side rails (2)	1-1/2 × 3-1/4 × 22-1/2
D	Side panels (6)	1/2 × 5 × 10-1/4
E	Front rail	1-1/2 × 3-1/4 × 24
F	Back stiles (2)	3/4 × 3 × 24
G	Back top rail	3/4 × 3 × 15-1/2
H	Back bottom rail	3/4 × 3 × 15-1/2
J	Slats (3)	3/8 × 2-1/2 × 19
K	Back supports (2)	3/4 × 3/4 × 8
L	Back cleat	1-1/4 × 2 × 21-1/2
M	Front cleat	1-1/4 × 1-1/2 × 19
N	Side cleats (2)	1-1/4 × 1-1/2 × 17-1/2
	Dowels	1/4 dia. × 2
	Dowels	3/8 dia. × 2
	Flathead wood screws	#10 × 2-1/4
	Flathead wood screws	#8 × 1-3/4
	Flathead wood screws	#8 × 1-1/4
	Panhead wood screws	#6 × 3/4
	Tacks	
	Dowel plugs or wood putty	
	Band irons	
	Rubber webbing	
	Wood glue	

#6 × 3/4" panhead screws. Do not screw the irons tight against the cleats; leave a 1/16" gap to pull the rubber webbing through.

16. Mark the proper spacing of the rubber webbing strips. Starting on one side, pull one strip through, double the end over, and tack fast. Repeat for each strip.

17. Stretch the strips across to the other side, and feed the end between the iron and cleat. Pull tight, then double the ends over and tack. Repeat this procedure for stretching the strips from front to back. Remember to interweave the webbing as shown.

18. Buy or make cushions to fit the armchair.

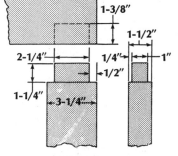

DETAIL A
BLIND MORTISE AND TENON

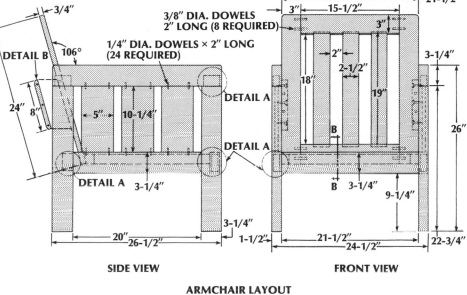

SIDE VIEW   FRONT VIEW

ARMCHAIR LAYOUT

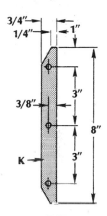

DETAIL B

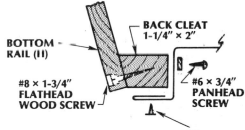

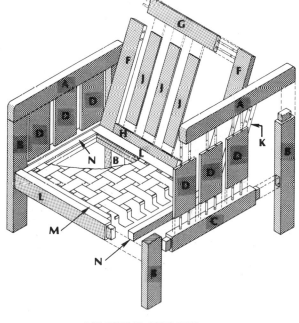

ARMCHAIR ASSEMBLY

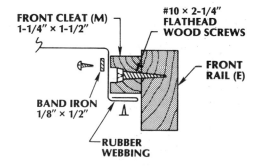

SECTION B-B
INNER FRAME DETAIL

to be a welcome addition to your dining room or kitchen.

1. Cut all pieces to size according to the dimensions given.

2. Drill 3/8"-diameter dowel holes in the legs, side rails (D) and end rails (C), as shown.

3. Construct the frame (C, E, F) using 6d finishing nails, then nail and glue the top (A) in place. Be sure to fill all nail holes with wood putty.

4. Assemble the legs and side rails (D) with 3/8"-diameter × 2" dowels, glue, and screws (see Detail A).

NOTE: Steps 5 and 6 deal with tables that have extensions.

5. The extension table has shorter end rails (C) to allow the extension supports (G) to extend out from the ends. The supports receive the extensions as shown.

6. Drill four 9/16"-diameter holes in each extension support and matching holes in the brackets (H). When the supports are mounted to the brackets in the extended position, use two or more 1/4" × 2" stove bolts with wing nuts to secure each support.

7. Sand all surfaces. Cover with plastic laminate or finish to suit your taste.

This parsons table offers a surface area of 19-1/4 square feet. By adding two table extensions, you can increase the surface area to more than 32 square feet. Either way you choose to build it, the table is sure

LIST OF MATERIALS
(Table without Extensions)

(finished dimensions in inches)

A	Top	3/4 × 42 × 66
B	Legs (4)	3 × 3 × 28-1/4
C	End rails (2)	3/4 × 2-1/4 × 36
D	Side rails (2)	3/4 × 2-1/4 × 60
E	Inner rails (2)	3/4 × 2-1/4 × 64-1/2
F	Center rail	3/4 × 2-1/4 × 34-1/2
	Dowels	3/8 dia. × 2
	Flathead wood screws	#10 × 2
	Roundhead wood screws	#10 × 2
	6d finishing nails	
	Wood putty	
	Wood glue	

LIST OF MATERIALS
(Table with Extensions)

(finished dimensions in inches)

A	Top	3/4 × 42 × 66
B	Legs (4)	3 × 3 × 28-1/4
C	End rails (2)	3/4 × 2-1/4 × 32-7/8
D	Side rails (2)	3/4 × 2-1/4 × 60
E	Inner rails (2)	3/4 × 2-1/4 × 66
F	Center rail	3/4 × 2-1/4 × 34-1/2
G	Extension supports (4)	3/4 × 2-1/4 × 32-3/4
H	Brackets (8)	3/4 × 2 × 16
J	Extension side rails (2)	3/4 × 2-1/4 × 42
K	Extension end rails (4)	3/4 × 2-1/4 × 22-1/4
L	Extension tops (2)	3/4 × 23 × 42
	Dowels	3/8 dia. × 2
	Stove bolts	1/4 dia. × 2
	Washers and wing nuts	1/4 dia.
	Roundhead wood screws	#10 × 1-1/2
	6d finishing nails	
	Wood putty	
	Wood glue	

**FRAME ASSEMBLY DIAGRAM
(WITHOUT EXTENSION)**

**FRAME ASSEMBLY DIAGRAM
(WITH EXTENSION)**

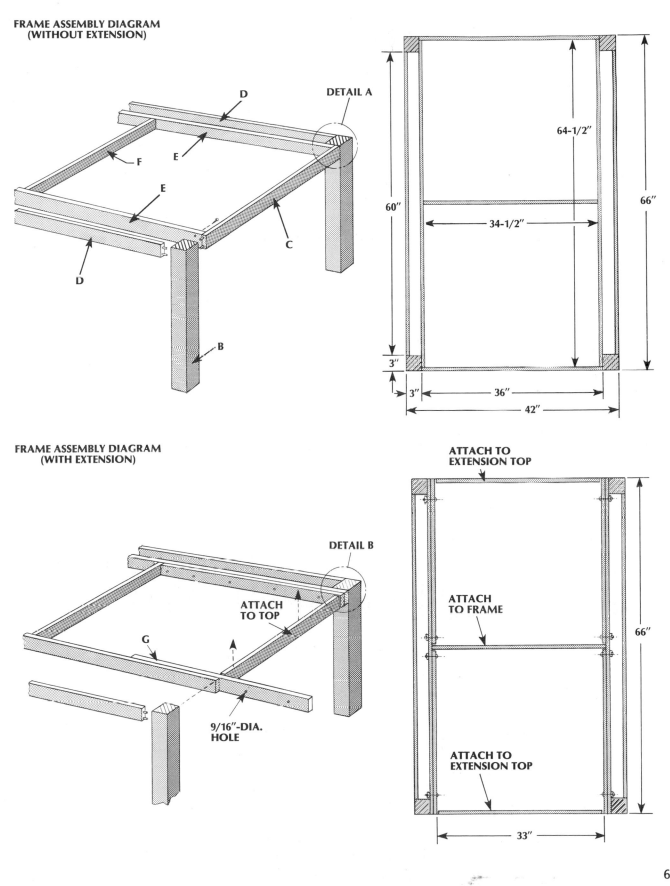

DETAIL A

D

E

F

E

D

C

B

64-1/2″

60″

34-1/2″

66″

3″

3″

36″

42″

DETAIL B

ATTACH
TO TOP

G

9/16″-DIA.
HOLE

ATTACH TO
EXTENSION TOP

ATTACH
TO FRAME

66″

ATTACH TO
EXTENSION TOP

33″

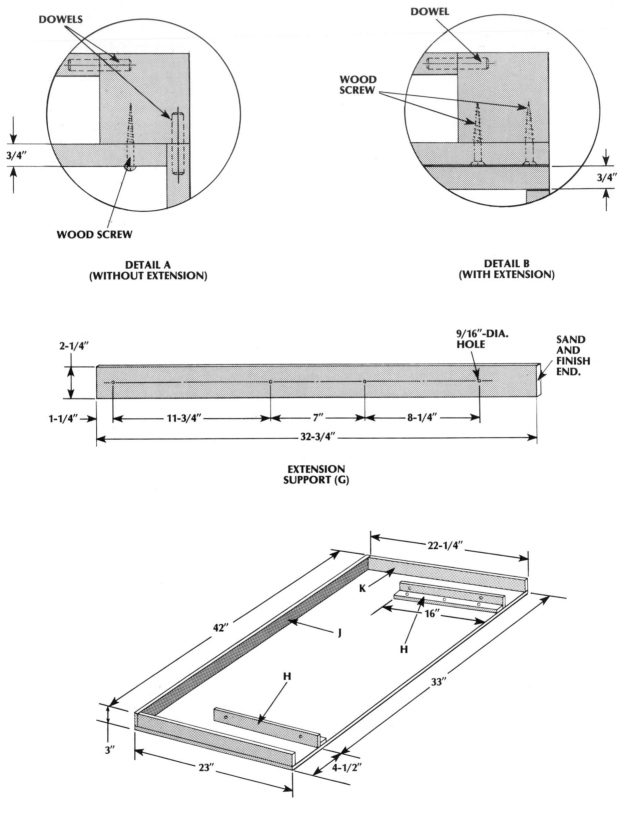

DOWELS

3/4"

WOOD SCREW

**DETAIL A
(WITHOUT EXTENSION)**

DOWEL

**WOOD
SCREW**

3/4"

**DETAIL B
(WITH EXTENSION)**

2-1/4"

**9/16"-DIA.
HOLE**

**SAND
AND
FINISH
END.**

1-1/4"   **11-3/4"**   **7"**   **8-1/4"**

32-3/4"

**EXTENSION
SUPPORT (G)**

22-1/4"

K

16"

42"

J

H

33"

H

3"

23"

4-1/2"

EXTENSION DETAIL

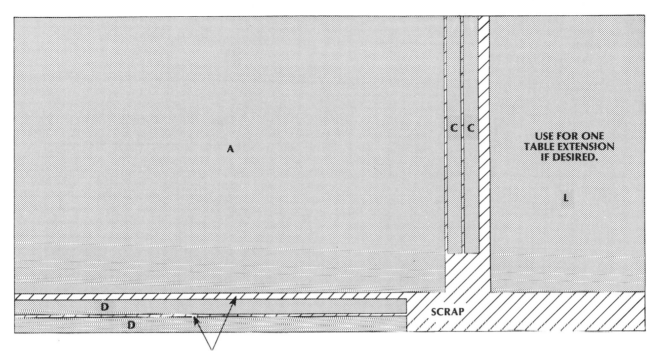

USE FOR ONE
TABLE EXTENSION
IF DESIRED.

SCRAP

NOTE: AMPLE ALLOWANCE NEEDED FOR SAW KERF.

3/4″ × 4′ × 8′ PLYWOOD CUTTING LAYOUT

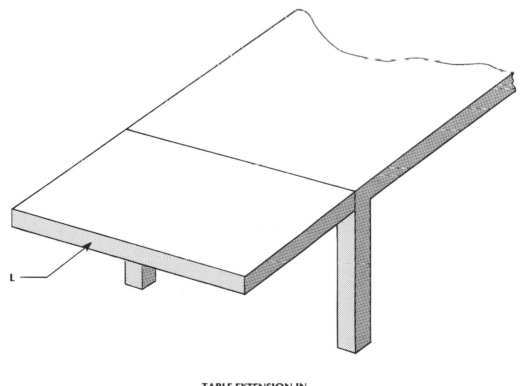

**TABLE EXTENSION IN
MOUNTED POSITION**

The basic design of this twin bed is very simple and sturdy. While templates are provided for the headboard and footboard, you can create your own pattern if you prefer. In fact, it might be a good idea to select a mattress first and then adjust the dimensions to fit.

1. Make full-size templates for the headboard (A) and footboard (B) using the patterns provided.

2. Glue up a pair of panels for the headboard and footboard from 2 × 6 and/or 2 × 8 stock. When the glue has dried, sand the panels smooth and cut them to the dimensions given.

3. Transfer the template designs to the panels. Cut out the headboard and footboard pieces, then sand their edges smooth.

4. Cut the remaining pieces to size using the dimensions provided.

5. Attach a sideboard support (E) to each foot (C) using flathead wood screws. Make two right-facing feet and two left-facing feet.

6. Fasten the feet to the headboard and footboard using glue and #10 × 2-1/2" flathead wood screws. Drive the screws counterbored through the boards into the edges of the feet. Counterbore the holes and plug them to hide the screw heads.

7. Attach a slat support (G) to the bottom inside edge of each sideboard (D) by driving screws through the support into the sideboard. Counterbore the screws for extra holding power.

8. Attach the sideboards to the feet, resting the sideboards on the supports inside the feet. Use four flathead wood screws at each corner, fastening from the inside. Do not use glue.

9. Add the slats (F), sand the entire bed, and finish as desired.

LIST OF MATERIALS

(finished dimensions in inches)

A	Headboard	1-1/2 × 38 × 44
B	Footboard	1-1/2 × 32 × 44
C	Feet (4)	1-1/2 × 5-1/2 × 16
D	Sideboards (2)	1-1/2 × 7-1/4 × 75
E	Sideboard supports (4)	1-1/2 × 3-1/2 × 6-3/4
F	Slats (5)	3/4 × 3-1/2 × 38
G	Slat supports (2)	1-1/2 × 1-1/2 × 75
	Flathead wood screws	#10 × 2-1/2
	Wood glue	

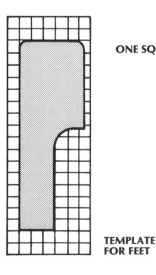

TEMPLATE FOR FEET

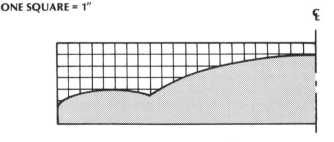

ONE SQUARE = 1"

TEMPLATE FOR HEADBOARD AND FOOTBOARD (UPPER EDGE)

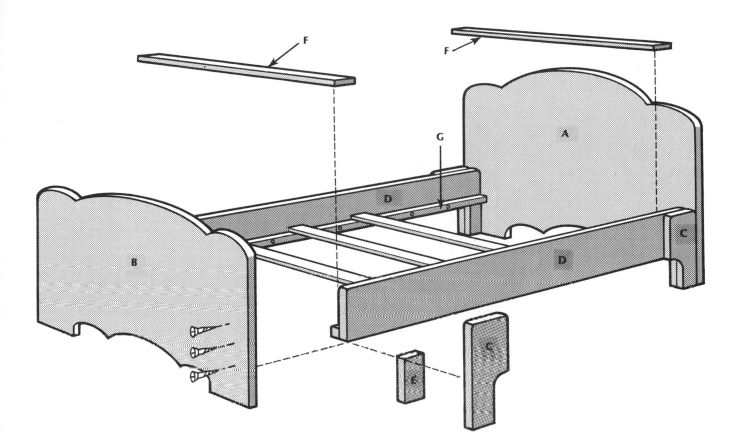

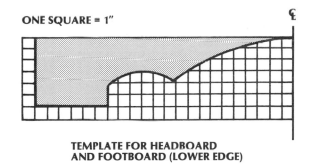

ONE SQUARE = 1"

**TEMPLATE FOR HEADBOARD
AND FOOTBOARD (LOWER EDGE)**

Here is a basic table design that can accommodate many uses. The table shown in the photo was made of redwood and assembled using waterproof glue and galvanized fasteners. Because it was designed to serve as a deck table, it is somewhat low in height. However, you can easily substitute other woods, use standard glue and fasteners, and raise the column height a few inches to create a handsome reading or dining table for the interior of your home.

1. Use the pattern provided to make a template for the feet (B), then lay them out on the lumber. By alternating directions and overlapping the feet, you can cut them out of 2 × 8 stock with minimal waste.

2. Form the top (D) by edge-gluing three pieces of 2 × 8 stock (or more numerous pieces of narrower stock). After the glue dries, sand the panel flat and trim it to the finished dimensions given in the list. Round over all edges with a router.

3. Cut the remaining parts to the dimensions provided.

4. Arrange the column sides (A) with their edges chasing each other, then fasten them into square columns using wood glue and 3d finishing nails. Set the nails just below the surface.

5. On the stretcher face of each column, center and drill a pair of 5/16"-diameter pilot holes, one 2-1/2" and the other 5" from the bottom. Center and drill a pair of holes of the same diameter through the remaining faces of each column; locate these holes 1" and 3-1/2" from the bottom.

6. Center and drill a pair of 7/32"-diameter pilot holes into each end of the stretcher(C) and into the back of each foot, using the same 2-1/2" center-to-center spacing used on the columns. Set the lower holes in the feet 1" above the bottom edge of their backs as indicated in the template pattern. Lo-

cate the holes in the stretcher 1" up from the bottom and 1" down from the top edges. Drill these holes as deep as necessary for installing the lag-thread ends of the hanger bolts.

7. Lag the hanger bolts into the feet and the stretcher, then fasten these parts to the two columns. Secure the bolts with lock washers and nuts.

8. Center the top brackets (E) over the column tops and fasten them in place using #8 × 1-1/2 flathead wood screws.

9. Lay the top upside down on a flat surface. Miter the ends of the apron pieces (F, G), then arrange them in a rectangle on the underside of the top. Make sure the apron is centered along the length and width.

10. Fasten the apron to the top using #10 × 2-1/2" countersunk flathead wood screws. Avoid using glue in this assembly since both the top and apron will tend to expand and contract with changing humidity.

11. Center the apron/top assembly over the leg/column assembly. Fasten them together by driving #8 × 1-1/2" flathead wood screws through the brackets into the top. (You will find this easier to do with the entire assembly turned upside down.)

12. Sand the table and finish according to taste.

LIST OF MATERIALS

(finished dimensions in inches)

A	Column sides (8)	3/4 × 3-1/2 × 14
B	Feet (6)	1-1/2 × 5-1/2 × 8-1/2
C	Stretcher	1-1/2 × 3-1/2 × 19
D	Top	1-1/2 × 21-1/2 × 44
E	Top brackets (2)	3/4 × 7-1/4 × 7-1/4
F	End aprons (2)	1-1/2 × 3-1/2 × 18-1/2
G	Side aprons (2)	1-1/2 × 3-1/2 × 41
	Hanger bolts (with nuts and lock washers)	1/4 dia. × 2-1/2
	Wood screws	#8 × 1-1/2
	Wood screws	#10 × 2-1/2
	3d finishing nails	
	Wood glue	

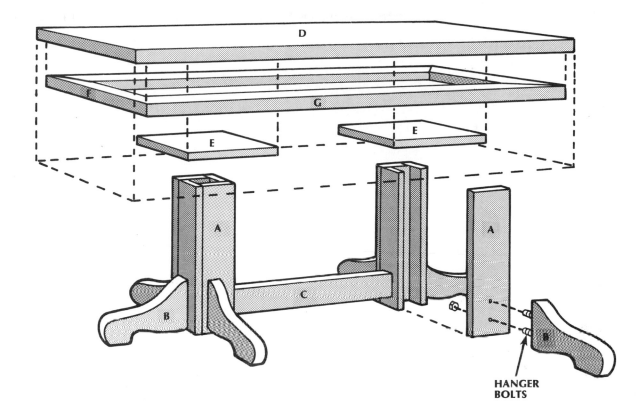

D

F

G

E

E

A

B

C

A

B

HANGER
BOLTS

ONE SQUARE = 1"

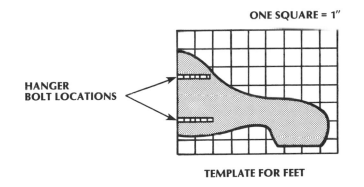

HANGER
BOLT LOCATIONS

TEMPLATE FOR FEET

This table will add beauty and convenience to any setting, indoors or out. The one shown here was made of redwood and assembled with waterproof fasteners. However, you can use the wood of your choice with conventional fasteners to create a lovely piece of indoor furniture. Adjust the column height and top dimensions to suit your tastes.

1. Cut the pieces to size according to the dimensions provided. Use the pattern to make a template for the feet (E).

2. Glue and screw or nail one edge of the column sides (A) at a time until the column is complete. Check for squareness.

3. Glue up the top (B) from 2 × 8 or narrower stock. After the glue dries, sand the panel flat and cut it to 21-1/2" square. Round over all sharp edges.

4. Cut 45° miters on the ends of the apron pieces (D). Center the pieces on the underside of the top, and drive #10 × 2-1/2" screws from underneath the apron into the top to secure.

5. Center the top bracket (C) on the column, and glue and screw it in place.

6. Center the top/apron assembly on the column, gluing and screwing from underneath through the top bracket.

7. Attach the feet to the column using hanger bolts and nuts.

8. Sand and finish as desired.

LIST OF MATERIALS

(finished dimensions in inches)

A	Column sides (4)	3/4 × 3-1/2 × 16
B	Top	1-1/2 × 21-1/2 × 21-1/2
C	Top bracket	3/4 × 7-1/4 × 7-1/4
D	Apron (4)	1-1/2 × 3-1/2 × 20-1/4
E	Feet (4)	1-1/2 × 5-1/2 × 8-1/2
	Hanger bolts, nuts, and lock washers	1/4 dia. × 2-1/2
	Wood screws	#10 × 2-1/2
	Wood screws	#8 × 1-1/2
	3d finishing nails	
	Wood glue	

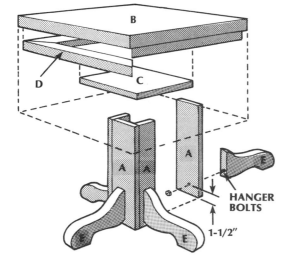

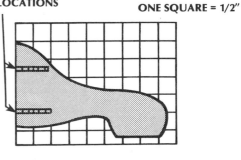

TEMPLATE FOR FEET

HANGER BOLT LOCATIONS

ONE SQUARE = 1/2"

This multi-purpose table drops flush to the wall when not in use. The hinged legs fold out of sight when the table is down, and you can even mount it on a wall to use it as a serving table.

1. Cut the pieces to size according to the dimensions given.

2. Nail the top pieces (A) to the top supports (B), then add the sides (C) and ends (D).

3. Attach the legs (F) with carriage bolts. Use a washer between the leg and the table at the pivot point so the leg can swing up properly for storage.

4. Mount hinges to the table and hinge piece (E). Attach the hinge piece to the wall at the proper leg height as shown.

5. Finish the table according to individual preference.

LIST OF MATERIALS

(finished dimensions in inches)

A	Top pieces (7)	3/4 × 3-1/2 × 46-1/2
B	Top supports (4)	3/4 × 3-1/2 × 24-1/2
C	Sides (2)	3/4 × 3-1/2 × 48
D	Ends (2)	3/4 × 3-1/2 × 24-1/2
E	Hinge piece	3/4 × 3-1/2 × 48
F	Legs (2)	3/4 × 3-1/2 × 30
	Carriage bolts and washers	1/4 dia. × 3-1/4
	3d finishing nails	
	Collapsible leg supports	

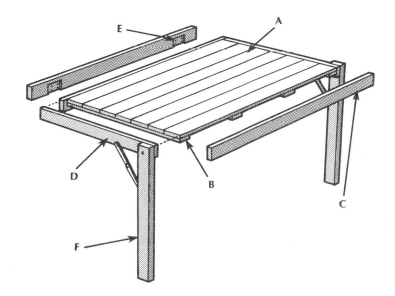

Any home handyman knows the value of a workbench. This one provides plenty of work space, a large shelf, and a perforated pegboard backing for hanging tools. The tabletop is made of 3/4" waferboard covered with 1/4" hardboard. The workbench shown here is 8' long, but you can make it any length to fit your work space.

1. Cut all pieces to size according to the dimensions given.

2. Assemble the support frames (F) for the tabletop (B) and the shelf (J) by fastening the fronts and backs to the crosspieces (G) using 12d nails. In both cases, position one crosspiece at each end and one across the middle. Add two more crosspieces to the top frame to help stiffen the tabletop work surface.

3. Cut a 3-1/2"-wide × 3/8"-deep rabbet across the top of each front leg (D) for fitting the top frame on the legs. Then cut dadoes of the same dimensions at a parallel location across each of the back legs (E). Also, cut parallel dadoes across each leg about 8" above the bottom for fitting the shelf frame between the legs.

4. Fasten the legs to the frames using #8 × 2-1/2" flathead wood screws countersunk flush with the leg surface. Use at least two screws per joint and offset them for increased frame stability.

LIST OF MATERIALS

(finished dimensions in inches)

A	Tabletop base	3/4 × 24 × 96 waferboard
B	Tabletop	1/4 × 24 × 96 hardboard
C	Backing	1/4 × 48 × 96 perforated hardboard
D	Front legs (3)	1-1/2 × 3-1/2 × 36
E	Back legs (3)	1-1/2 × 3-1/2 × 83-1/2
F	Top and shelf frame fronts and backs (4)	1-1/2 × 3-1/2 × 93
G	Top and shelf frame crosspieces (8)	1-1/2 × 3-1/2 × 19-1/2
H	Crossbar	1-1/2 × 1-1/2 × 93
J	Shelf	3/4 × 23-7/8 × 93 waferboard
	Wood screws	#6 × 7/8
	Wood screws	#8 × 1-1/2
	Wood screws	#8 × 2-1/2
	Angle irons	1-1/2 or 2
	12d nails	
	Construction adhesive	

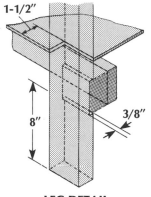

LEG DETAIL

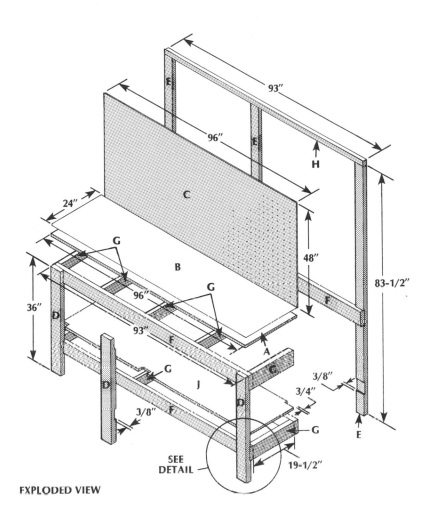

EXPLODED VIEW

5. Cut 3-1/2"-wide × 1-1/2"-deep notches in the front edge of the shelf, one at each end and one in the middle, in order to fit the shelf around the front legs. Cut parallel notches of the same width, but 3/4" in depth, on the back edge of the shelf for fitting around the back legs.

6. Insert the shelf between the legs and fasten it to the support frame using #8 × 1-1/2" flathead wood screws, countersunk flush or driven slightly below the shelf surface. If you like, run a bead of construction adhesive along the upper edge of the frame before installing the shelf.

7. Set the tabletop base (A) on the top frame. Push the top against the back legs and center it along the length of the support frame.

8. Clamp or tack the top in place while drilling countersunk pilot holes for #8 screws through it into the frame. Space the holes about 12" apart. If you want to use construction adhesive, remove the top and spread a bead of adhesive on the top of the frame. Then reposition the top and fasten it in place using #8 × 1-1/2" flathead wood screws. Drive all the screws slightly below the surface of the tabletop.

9. Position the tabletop over the base, making all edges flush. Then fasten the top to the base using #6 × 7/8" flathead wood screws, driven slightly below the outer surface. This installation method will allow for periodic replacement of

the tabletop. For permanent installation, apply construction adhesive to the base, position the tabletop over it, and press it flat, then tack it in place.

10. Place the bench in the desired location and shim the legs as needed to make the top completely level and to stabilize the bench. Then use angle irons to fasten the legs to the floor, or run fasteners through the back legs into the wall, or do both.

11. Set the backing (C) on the tabletop. Center it along the length of the bench, then fasten it to the upper section of the back legs and to the crossbar (H) using #6 × 7/8" flathead wood screws.

GATELEG TABLE

This gateleg table is elegant enough for indoor dining, yet light enough to be carried outdoors when the occasion arises. It opens up to a surface area large enough to accommodate four people and is the perfect project to show off your craftsmanship.

1. Cut the pieces to size according to the dimensions given.
2. Cut 1/2"-deep × 3-1/2"-wide rabbets on the tops of the legs (A). On the same side of each leg, cut 1/2"-deep × 2-1/2"-wide dadoes 3" up from the bottom.
3. Round and sand the edges of the legs and the back sides of the long bottom and top stretchers (B, C).
4. Assemble the two large frames using glue and wood screws. Round over the edges and sand the faces of the frames.
5. Cut 3/4"-deep × 1-1/2"-wide rabbets in the ends of the short bottom and top stretchers (D, E).
6. Assemble the four small frames, using glue and two screws at each joint. The stretchers should lap the legs and protrude 1/4". Counterbore and plug the holes; then round over the edges and sand the faces of the frames.
7. Fasten one small frame to the left side of each large frame. The leg on the small frame should sit against the leg on the large frame as shown. To do this, drive two screws from the back through the stretcher into the top and bottom of each leg.
8. Cut 3/4"-deep × 1-1/2"-wide laps in the ends of the bottom and top side stretchers (F, G). Sand the stretchers; then attach them to the frames using glue and screws. Plug the screw holes.
9. Attach the two remaining small frames to the base using butt hinges. This completes the base of the table.
10. Glue up stock for the top and leaf pieces (H, J). The top will overhang the base 1-1/4" on each side to accommodate the hinges.
11. Mount the top to the base by screwing and plugging through the top into the stretchers.
12. Use three hinges to attach each leaf to the top, making sure that the center hinge is in front of the stationary frame so it will not interfere with the movement of the gate leg.
13. Sand the entire table and finish as desired.

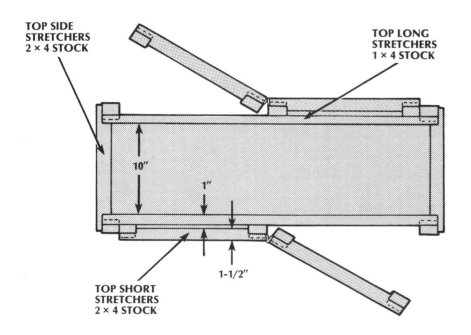

TOP SIDE
STRETCHERS
2 × 4 STOCK

TOP LONG
STRETCHERS
1 × 4 STOCK

10"

1"

1-1/2"

TOP SHORT
STRETCHERS
2 × 4 STOCK

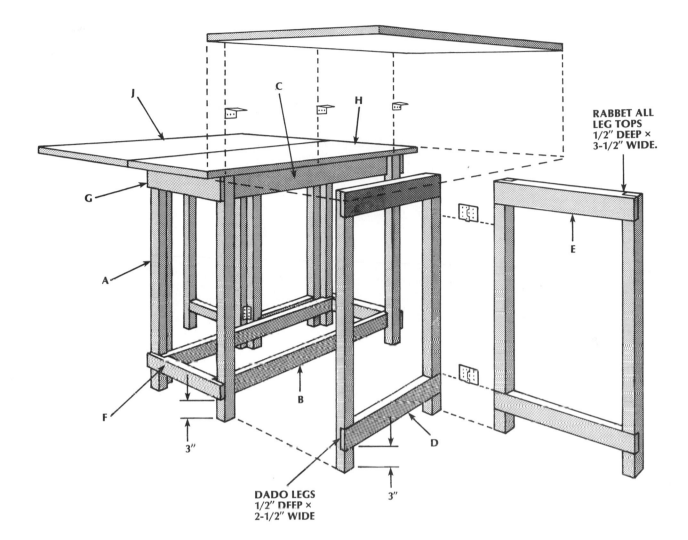

RABBET ALL LEG TOPS 1/2" DEEP × 3-1/2" WIDE.

DADO LEGS 1/2" DEEP × 2-1/2" WIDE

3"

3"

LIST OF MATERIALS

(finished dimensions in inches)

A	Legs (12)	1-1/2 × 1-1/2 × 28-1/2
B	Bottom long stretchers (2)	3/4 × 2-1/2 × 38-1/4
C	Top long stretchers (2)	3/4 × 3-1/2 × 38-1/4
D	Bottom short stretchers (4)	1-1/2 × 2-1/2 × 17-1/2
E	Top short stretchers (4)	1-1/2 × 3-1/2 × 17-1/2
F	Bottom side stretchers (2)	1-1/2 × 2-1/2 × 13
G	Top side stretchers (2)	1-1/2 × 3-1/2 × 13
H	Top	3/4 × 17-1/2 × 47-1/2
J	Leaves (2)	3/4 × 18-1/2 × 47-1/2
	Wood screws	#8 × 1
	Tabletop fasteners	
	Brass butt hinges (7)	1-1/2 × 2
	Wood plugs	
	Wood glue	

the nails and fill the holes with matching wood putty.

6. Angle-cut the ends of the top rails (E) as shown.

7. Assemble the narrow inside frames first. Begin by locating and drilling 1/4"-diameter dowel holes 1" deep at the joints for the legs (D) and top and bottom rails (E, G).

8. On the outside of the narrow frame legs, drill 1/4"-diameter holes 1" deep exactly 17" from the bottom of the legs. This is the location of the pivot pins for folding the stand.

9. Glue the pivot pins in place, then assemble the narrow frame. Glue the dowel joints and clamp until dry. Check for squareness.

10. Drill 1/4"-diameter holes 1" deep exactly 17" from the bottom of the inside of the large frame legs. Assemble the top and bottom (F) rails and one side of the large frame.

11. Insert the small frame inside the large frame, lining up the pivot pins in the frame holes. Do not glue pins in the large frame legs.

12. Position and glue the remaining outside frame leg in place. Sand all stand parts at the joints and the surface.

13. Finish with clear polyurethane finish. When dry, you might want to tack or staple fabric strapping to the underside of the top rails so the frame opens up to 24" in width.

This generously sized tray can be used separately or placed permanently on the folding stand. The classic design and rich walnut goes well with either contemporary or country furnishings.

1. Cut all stock to size according to the dimensions provided.

2. Glue up random width stock to make the tray bottom (C) slightly oversized. When the glue has dried, sand on both sides and trim the bottom to final size.

3. Miter the corners for connecting the back (A) and the tray sides (B). Cut 1/4"-wide × 1/2"-deep rabbets on the lower inside edges of the back and sides. Taper the inner face on each piece down to 3/8" thickness, beginning the taper at the top of the rabbet as shown.

4. Drill and cut out the handholes on the tray sides as shown.

5. Final sand the tray pieces, including the handholes. Assemble the tray using glue and 4d finishing nails at the corners, and glue and 2d finishing nails through the bottom into the sides. Predrill all nail holes for easier construction; set

LIST OF MATERIALS

(finished dimensions in inches)

A	Back	3/4 × 5 × 30
B	Tray sides (2)	3/4 × 5 × 16-1/4
C	Tray bottom	1/2 × 16 × 29
D	Legs (4)	3/4 × 1-3/4 × 34-1/4
E	Top rails (2)	3/4 × 1-3/4 × 16
F	Bottom rail	3/4 × 1-3/4 × 10-1/2
G	Bottom rail	3/4 × 1-3/4 × 7
	Grooved dowel pivot pins	1/4 dia. × 2
	Fabric strapping	1-1/2 × 2 × 32
	2d finishing nails	
	4d finishing nails	
	Wood putty	
	Wood glue	

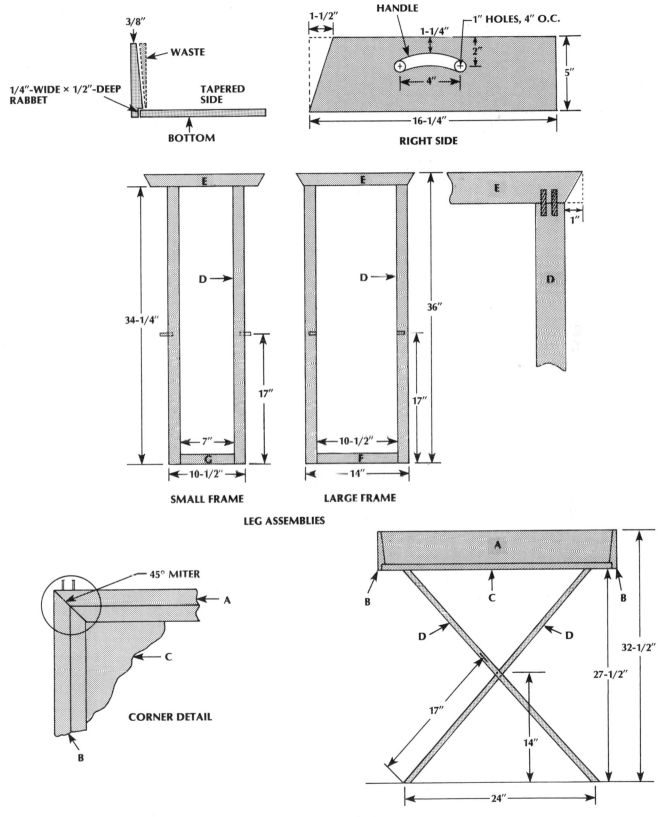

3/8″

WASTE

1/4″-WIDE × 1/2″-DEEP RABBET

TAPERED SIDE

BOTTOM

HANDLE

1-1/2″

1-1/4″

1″ HOLES, 4″ O.C.

2″

4″

5″

16-1/4″

RIGHT SIDE

E

D

34-1/4″

17″

7″

10-1/2″

SMALL FRAME

G

E

D

36″

17″

10-1/2″

14″

LARGE FRAME

F

E

D

1″

LEG ASSEMBLIES

45° MITER

A

C

B

CORNER DETAIL

A

B

C

B

D

D

32-1/2″

27-1/2″

17″

14″

24″

FRONT VIEW

Smart gardeners don't wait for the ground to thaw and the air to warm before starting their spring gardening. The first seeds are always sown inside the house in a spot that gets plenty of sunshine. Unfortunately, space is usually a limiting factor in most seed starting operations. Only a few windows normally get sufficient sunshine to produce healthy seedlings, and there never seems to be enough window ledge to satisfy your aspirations. However, you can expand your preseason gardening space with the suspended seed starter shown here.

This four-tiered shelf unit is designed to be mounted into a standard window frame. The shelves, which are removable to facilitate larger plants, are supported by two metal side frames. The bottom shelf is designed to rest on the window sill; consequently, this and all other shelf dimensions must be sized to your particular window. The unit receives plenty of light, takes up no floor space, and can be dismounted easily when not in use. Tools, soil, and miscellaneous gardening materials are conveniently stored in the two drawers under the bottom shelf.

1. To begin building your indoor garden, start by cutting the bottom shelf back (A) to length. Cut a 1/2"-wide × 3/8"-deep groove in the back, one inch from the top edge, to hold the plywood bottom.

2. Cut the bottom shelf sides (B) to length. Cut a 1/2"-wide × 3/8"-deep groove in each side, one inch from the top edge, to hold the plywood shelf. Machine a 3/4"-wide × 3/8"-deep rabbet on the back inside end of each side piece. Make a right and left piece.

3. Cut a blind rabbet 3/4" wide × 3/8" deep × 1-1/2" long on the uncut end of each side to accept the bottom shelf front (D).

4. Cut the middle drawer support (C) and the drawer glides (E) to length. Glue and nail the drawer glides to the middle drawer support and the side pieces.

5. Cut the bottom shelf front to length. Cut a 1/2"-high × 3/8"-deep rabbet in the bottom inside edge to accept the plywood shelf.

6. Cut the bottom shelf (F) to size. Assemble the shelf unit parts using glue and 5d finishing nails.

7. Cut the drawer fronts (G) and sides (H) to length. Machine a 3/4"-wide × 3/8"-deep rabbet on each end of the drawer fronts to accept the drawer sides.

8. Machine a 1/4"-wide × 3/8"-deep groove on each drawer front to accept the drawer bottom, 1/4" from the bottom edge.

9. Machine the same 1/4" × 3/8" groove on each side piece. Cut a

LIST OF MATERIALS

(finished dimensions in inches)

A	Bottom shelf back	3/4 × 5-1/2 × 35-1/4
B	Bottom shelf sides (2)	3/4 × 5-1/2 × 18
C	Middle drawer support	3/4 × 4 × 17-1/4
D	Bottom shelf front	3/4 × 1-1/2 × 35-1/4
E	Drawer glides (4)	3/8 × 3/4 × 16-7/8
F	Bottom shelf	1/2 × 17-1/4 × 35-1/4 plywood
G	Drawer fronts (2)	3/4 × 4 × 16-7/8
H	Drawer sides (4)	3/4 × 4 × 16-7/8
J	Drawer backs (2)	3/4 × 3-1/2 × 16-1/8
K	Drawer bottoms (2)	1/4 × 16-1/8 × 16-7/8 plywood
L	Shelf fronts and backs (6)	3/4 × 1-1/2 × 35-1/4
M	Top shelf ends (2)	3/4 × 1-1/2 × 7
N	Middle shelf ends (2)	3/4 × 1-1/2 × 10-1/2
P	Lower shelf ends (2)	3/4 × 1-1/2 × 14
Q	Top shelf	1/4 × 6-1/4 × 35-1/4 plywood
R	Middle shelf	1/4 × 9-3/4 × 35-1/4 plywood
S	Lower shelf	1/4 × 13-1/4 × 35-1/4 plywood
	1/4"-dia. steel rod	
	Finishing nails	
	Roundhead wood screws	
	Clear silicone caulk	
	Wood glue	

3/4"-wide × 3/8"-deep groove on the outside face of each drawer side for the drawer glides.

10. Machine a 3/4"-wide × 3/8"-deep rabbet on the end of each side piece to accept the back panel.

11. Cut the drawer backs (J) and drawer bottoms (K) to size.

12. Assemble the drawer sides, front, back, and bottom with glue and nails. Note that the back must be installed flush at the top; also, the bottom cannot be glued; it must always be nailed.

13. Cut the top, middle, and lower shelf ends (M, N, P) to length. Machine a 3/4"-wide × 3/8"-deep rab-

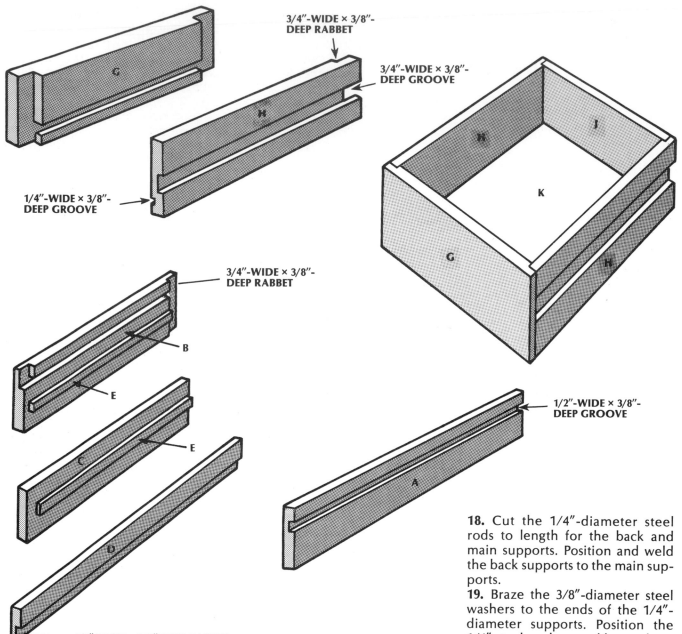

3/4"-WIDE × 3/8"-DEEP RABBET

3/4"-WIDE × 3/8"-DEEP GROOVE

1/4"-WIDE × 3/8"-DEEP GROOVE

3/4"-WIDE × 3/8"-DEEP RABBET

1/2"-WIDE × 3/8"-DEEP GROOVE

1/2"-HIGH × 3/8"-DEEP RABBET

bet on each end of the pieces. Machine a 1/4"-wide × 3/8"-deep groove 1/4" from the bottom edge of each piece.

14. Cut the shelf fronts and backs (L) to length. Machine a 1/4"-wide × 3/8"-deep groove 1/4" from the bottom edge of each piece.

15. Cut the top, middle, and lower shelf bottoms (Q, R, S) to size. Assemble all the shelf elements with glue and nails, except the bottom, which should not be glued.

16. Machine a 1/4" radius on all sharp edges of the shelf frames, or round them over with a sanding block.

17. Sand all surfaces and finish as desired; polyurethane varnish is recommended. Caulk the inside joints of the shelves with clear silicone caulking.

18. Cut the 1/4"-diameter steel rods to length for the back and main supports. Position and weld the back supports to the main supports.

19. Braze the 3/8"-diameter steel washers to the ends of the 1/4"-diameter supports. Position the 1/4" steel washers and braze them to the supports at the desired locations.

20. Wire brush the side frames to remove loose scale and dirt. Paint the side frames.

21. Attach the side frames to the shelf units. Use #12 × 3/4" roundhead wood screws for the top three shelves and #12 × 1-1/4" roundhead wood screws for the shelf with drawers.

22. Mount the unit to the window with #14 × 2-1/2" wood screws.

Here's the solution to uneven tables that constantly wobble: a three-legged triangular table. While the idea is a simple one, figuring out the angles provided a challenge. The result is a sturdy table with tapered legs that fit into mortises formed by bevels and compound miters. To build it, use the following step-by-step procedure:

1. Choose wood for this project that is both strong and stable. Ash and cherry were used in this example; the harder ash is ideal for the legs and leg mortises, with the cherry serving as a contrast in the areas of less strain.

2. Because the tapered legs (E) go entirely through the tabletop, the mortises into which they fit must be a particular angle and shape. The easiest way to accomplish this is to construct these angled mortises with beveled and angled parts to make up the tabletop. Begin construction by cutting out on a bandsaw the three isosceles triangles that form the inside of the tabletop (A).

3. Disc sand the triangles so they are identical, then mark the bottom of each one with an X. Cut 1/4"-wide × 1/2"-deep spline grooves on the two inside edges of each triangle, making sure that the X is kept away from the rip fence.

4. Glue and clamp the triangles together. After the glue has dried, use a disc sander to touch up the outside edges of this inner triangle.

5. The top middle pieces (B, C) also form the leg mortises. This means that each part must have one beveled edge, one mitered end, and one compound mitered end. First, cut three pieces of stock that measure 1-1/2" × 1-3/4" × 14".

6. Tilt the saw table 5° and bevel one edge of each board. Mark an X on the wide edge of each board to indicate the bottom side. Now return the table to 0°, set the miter gauge at 60°, and miter one end of each board.

7. Place the three boards (B) around the inner triangle and mark for length. With the miter gauge still set at 60°, tilt the table 14° and cut the opposite end of each board. The undersides should now be longer and wider than the tops.

8. Cut matching spline grooves in each of the boards, identical to those made in step 3. Glue and clamp the boards to the inner triangle.

9. To complete the leg mortises, cut three pieces of stock (C) that measure 1-1/2" × 1-5/8" × 20". Tilt the saw table 5° and bevel one edge of each piece. This bevel matches those made in step 6 on the shorter middle boards (B); the result is that these boards will be wider on the top than on the bottom.

10. Mark the lengths of the three boards from the assembled central section. With the table set at 5° and the miter gauge set at 60°, miter one end of each piece.

11. The final operation on these boards is to bevel the undersides. Tilt the table 30° and, with the 5° beveled side facing up, cut each board so it tapers from 1-1/2" thick on the beveled edge to 3/4" thick on the outside edge.

12. Glue and clamp the boards to the central assembly. When the glue has dried, disc sand the cor-

ners on the underside of the table to match the bevel.

13. Drill a 3/8"-diameter hole 3-1/2" deep through the long middle boards as shown, joint, and glue dowels in place to reinforce the joints.

14. The edge pieces (D) complete the top. Cut the pieces to size, then set the table at 0°. With the miter gauge set at 60°, miter one end of each piece.

15. Tilt the table 15° and bevel the bottom side of each piece, tapering the bottom from 3/4" down to a 1/2" edge.

16. Glue and clamp the edge pieces to the main assembly. With the bandsaw, cut off the corners and disc sand to the final dimension.

17. To make the legs (E), start with three 4"-wide pieces of 1-3/4"-thick stock. Tilt the table to 30° and adjust a tapering jig to cut a 2-1/2° taper on a 20"-long piece of stock. Mark an X on the top of each leg, then make one pass on each leg. Use a push stick for this to keep the wood secure.

18. Flip the stock over end for end; the X should now be on the underside of the legs. Move the rip fence about 1/2" closer to the blade; the triangle formed by the saw kerf and the blade should be 3/4" on each side.

19. Cut the remaining tapers, then test-fit the legs in the mortises. Mark the legs where they come through the bottom of the tabletop, then remove them. With the miter gauge set at 14°, disc sand the legs to equal length.

20. Apply glue to the legs and the mortises, then tap the legs in place. Cut off the top remainder of the legs with a handsaw.

21. Belt sand the top to make the tabletop surface flush. Finish as desired.

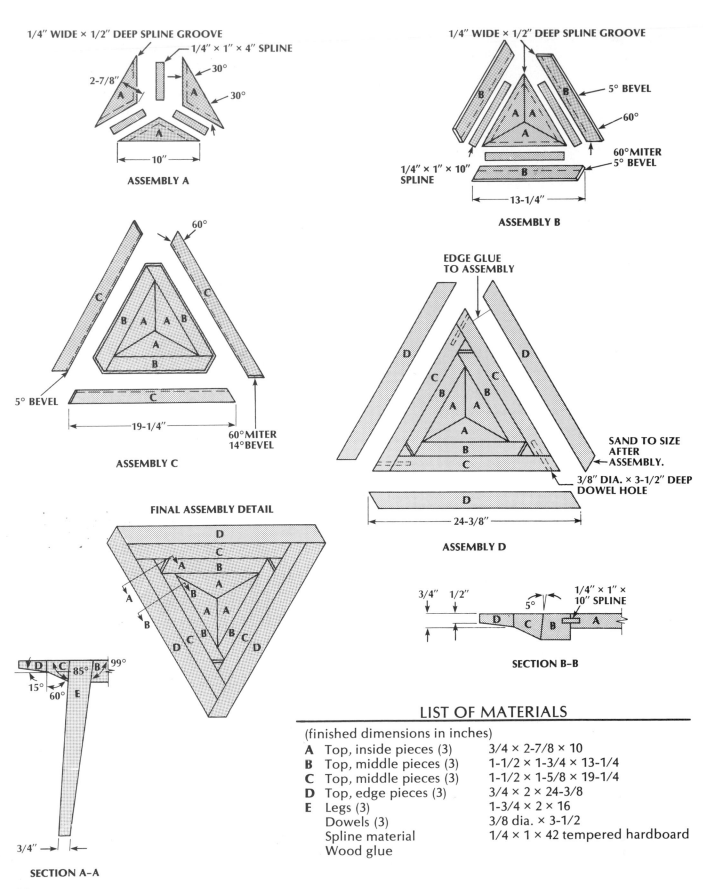

ASSEMBLY A

1/4" WIDE × 1/2" DEEP SPLINE GROOVE
1/4" × 1" × 4" SPLINE
2-7/8"
30°
30°
A
A
A
10"

ASSEMBLY B

1/4" WIDE × 1/2" DEEP SPLINE GROOVE
5° BEVEL
60°
B
B
A A
A
60° MITER
5° BEVEL
1/4" × 1" × 10" SPLINE
B
13-1/4"

ASSEMBLY C

60°
C
C
B A A B
A
B
5° BEVEL
C
19-1/4"
60° MITER
14° BEVEL

ASSEMBLY D

EDGE GLUE TO ASSEMBLY
D
D
C
C
B
B
A A
A
B
C
SAND TO SIZE AFTER ASSEMBLY.
3/8" DIA. × 3-1/2" DEEP DOWEL HOLE
D
24-3/8"

FINAL ASSEMBLY DETAIL

D
C
A
B
A
B
A
A
C
B B C
D D
A
B

SECTION A-A

D C 85° B 99°
15°
60°
E
3/4"

SECTION B-B

3/4" 1/2"
5°
1/4" × 1" × 10" SPLINE
D C B A

LIST OF MATERIALS

(finished dimensions in inches)

A	Top, inside pieces (3)	3/4 × 2-7/8 × 10
B	Top, middle pieces (3)	1-1/2 × 1-3/4 × 13-1/4
C	Top, middle pieces (3)	1-1/2 × 1-5/8 × 19-1/4
D	Top, edge pieces (3)	3/4 × 2 × 24-3/8
E	Legs (3)	1-3/4 × 2 × 16
	Dowels (3)	3/8 dia. × 3-1/2
	Spline material	1/4 × 1 × 42 tempered hardboard
	Wood glue	

Glue and clamp triangles together.

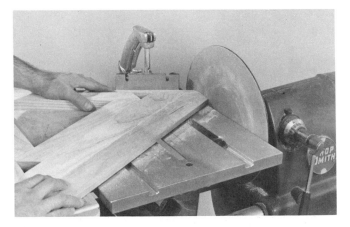

With bandsaw, cut off corners and disc sand to final dimension.

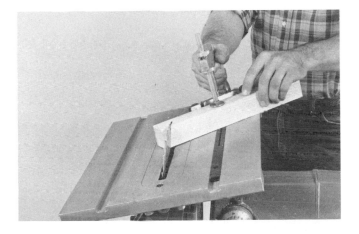

With miter gauge set at 60°, tilt table 14° and cut other end of each part. (Saw guard removed for clarity only.)

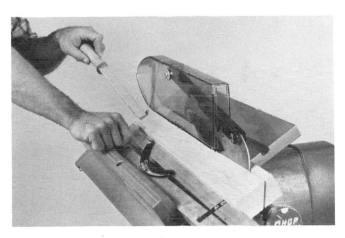

Make one pass on each leg.

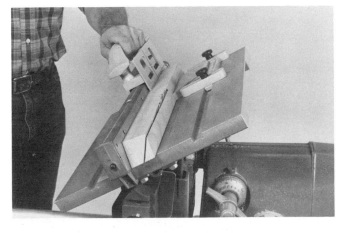

Cut stock so it tapers from 1-1/2" thick on beveled edge to 3/4" thick on outside edge. (Saw guard removed for clarity only.)

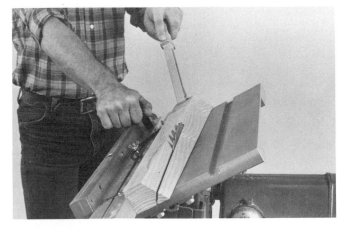

Triangle formed by saw kerf and blade should be 3/4" on each side. (Saw guard removed for clarity only.)

1. Cut all the pieces to size.
2. Round the front edges of the top and bottom end pieces (B) on a jigsaw or bandsaw.
3. Drill a 1/2"-diameter hole, 3/8" deep, in the middle of the top surface of the bottom end piece and the bottom surface of the top end piece. NOTE: Drill the holes about 2" away from the back edge to allow the horizontal pieces (C) to pivot without hitting the wall piece (A).
4. Drill a 1/2" hole through the center of each horizontal piece, 1" from the back edge for insertion of the support dowel (D).
5. Cut a 3/8"-deep × 3/4"-wide rabbet on the back edge of the top and bottom end pieces for joining to the wall piece.
6. Cut a tapering chamfer on all four edges of each horizontal piece. Start the chamfer 5" in from the back edge of the piece, increasing the taper to a full 1/4" at the front edge.
7. Drill dowel holes in the support dowel at the desired positions underneath the horizontal pieces (as shown).
8. Sand all pieces. If the support dowel fits too tightly, sand it. Do not redrill the holes or you risk making the horizontal pieces fit in a flimsy way.
9. Assemble the horizontal pieces on the support dowel, place the dowel in the holes in the top and bottom end pieces, then glue and nail the end and wall pieces together.
10. Finish as desired.

Whether or not you are an herb gardener, you will enjoy the rustic flavor this herb drying rack will add to your kitchen. Designed after a much larger Shaker herb rack, this project can be used to display dried flowers, hanging pots, or whatever else your imagination can muster.

The rack is designed to be fastened to a wall. When not in use, the horizontal drying bars fold conveniently against the wall, out of the way of traffic. When in use for the summer herb harvest, it provides a handy place to hang bundles of herbs. Best of all, the simplicity of design allows this project to be completed in an afternoon, with basic hand or power tools. The dimensions can be lengthened or shortened to suit individual tastes.

LIST OF MATERIALS

(finished dimensions in inches)

A	Wall piece	3/4 × 3-1/2 × 23-3/4
B	End pieces (2)	3/4 × 3-1/2 × 4
C	Horizontal pieces (6)	3/4 × 1-1/4 × 20
D	Support dowel	1/2 dia. × 23-3/4
	1/8-dia. × 3/4 dowels	
	4d finishing nails	
	Wood glue	

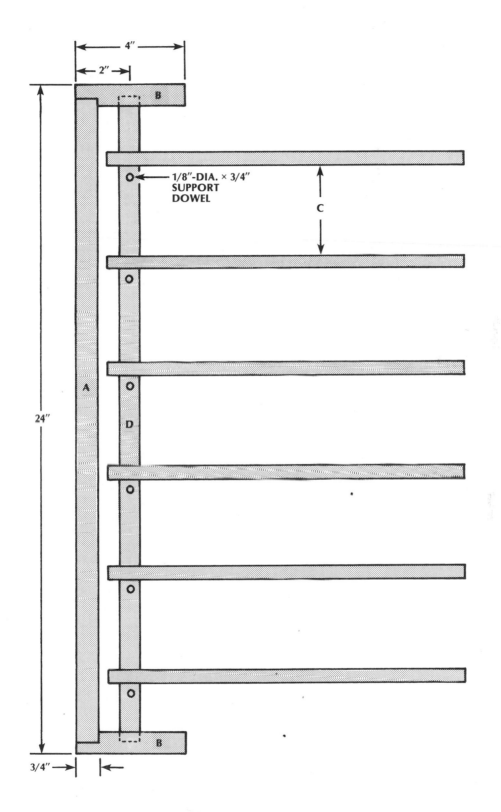

4"

2"

B

24"

1/8"-DIA. × 3/4"
SUPPORT
DOWEL

C

A

D

3/4"

B

The router is one of the most versatile tools in any workshop. There is little you cannot do with a router and the proper accessories. The router caddy shown here is designed to store your router on a pad so that the router bit does not have to be removed from the collet. Extra bits are displayed in the recessed door frames against a white background that makes identification easy. Three shelves are large enough to hold wrenches, guides, and other accessories.

The plans and dimensions given here are for a typical 1 to 1-1/2 horsepower router. If your router requires more or less space, adjust the dimensions to suit.

1. Begin by cutting the top and bottom (A) and sides (B) to length. Rabbet the top and bottom edge of the sides 3/4" wide and 3/8" deep.
2. Machine a 1/4" × 1/4" rabbet in the back edge of the sides, top, and bottom for the back panel. Dado the top and bottom along the centerline 3/4" × 3/8".
3. Cut the divider (C) and shelves (D) to length. Rip 1/4" from the back edge of each to allow room

for the back panel. Machine 3/4" × 3/8" dadoes in the divider and left side to accept the shelves.
4. Assemble the sides, top, bottom, divider, and shelves. Glue and nail together with 4d finishing nails.
5. Cut the back (E) to size and let into the back rabbet. Secure with glue and 4d finishing nails.

6. Cut the pads (F) to size and round the front edge using a 1/2" edge rounding router bit. Glue and nail to the bottom of the router compartment as shown. Sand and finish the caddy as desired.
7. Cut the 3/4" × 1" door frame members to size. Rabbet the stiles (G) to accept the rails (H) in a half-lap joint. Machine the notches 3/4" wide and 5/8" deep.
8. Machine 3/4" × 1/4" dadoes in the side frame members to accept the struts (J). Cut the struts to size and drill holes spaced 1" apart to accept the router bit shanks.
9. Cut the door panels (K) to size. Paint the inside of the door panels white.
10. Glue and nail the door frames together. Rout a 1/4" × 1/4" rabbet in the inside edge of the frame.
11. Square the corners and secure the door panel in the rabbet with glue and 2d finishing nails. Sand and finish as desired.
12. Mortise hinges into each door frame and into the caddy sides. Space the doors 1/8" apart and fasten to the caddy.
13. Attach magnetic catches and porcelain knobs. Hang the caddy at chest level.

LIST OF MATERIALS

(finished dimensions in inches)

A	Top and bottom (2)	3/4 × 7-1/4 × 21-1/2
B	Sides (2)	3/4 × 7-1/4 × 10-1/4
C	Divider	3/4 × 7 × 9-1/2
D	Shelves (2)	3/4 × 7 × 10-3/4
E	Back	1/4 × 10-3/4 × 21-1/2 plywood
F	Pads (2)	3/4 × 3-1/2 × 7
G	Stiles (4)	3/4 × 1 × 10-1/4
H	Rails (4)	3/4 × 1 × 10-1/16
J	Struts (4)	3/4 × 3/4 × 10-1/16
K	Door panels (2)	1/4 × 9-1/4 × 10-1/16
	2d finishing nails	
	4d finishing nails	
	2" butt hinges (4)	
	Porcelain knobs (2)	
	Magnetic latches (2)	
	Wood glue	

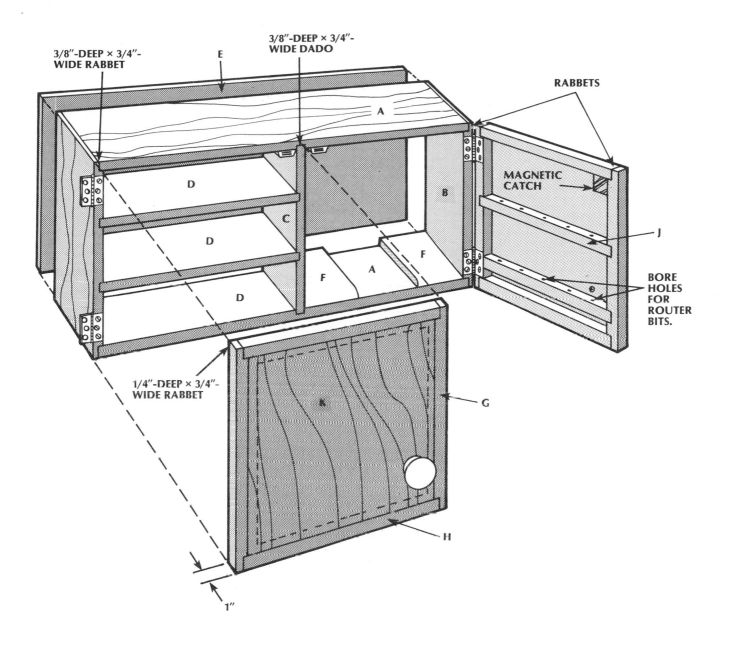

3/8"-DEEP × 3/4"-WIDE RABBET

3/8"-DEEP × 3/4"-WIDE DADO

E

RABBETS

A

B

MAGNETIC CATCH

D

C

D

J

D

F

A

F

BORE HOLES FOR ROUTER BITS.

1/4"-DEEP × 3/4"-WIDE RABBET

K

G

H

1"

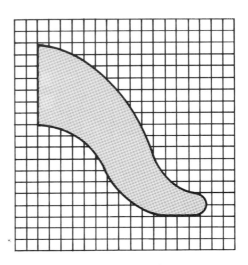

LEG PATTERN

ONE SQUARE = 1/2"

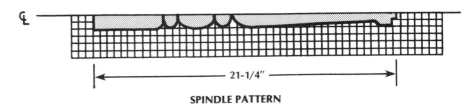

21-1/4"

SPINDLE PATTERN

6. Use a router with a 1/4" rounding over bit to shape the curved edges of the legs. Do not shape the straight sections.

7. On the drum sander, sand a concave curve in the straight portion of the legs. This will provide a better fit when attaching the legs to the spindle.

8. Mark and drill two 3/8"-diameter holes in the spindle base as shown to accommodate the dowels. Glue the legs to the spindle, one at a time, and allow each leg time to set up. Make sure the bottoms of the legs are square to the outside of the spindle.

9. Glue and clamp the stock for the top (B). When the glue has dried, lay out the 16"-diameter circle and cut it out using a scroll saw, bandsaw, or jigsaw.

10. Disc sand the edges of the top. The top edge can be shaped with a router and a roman ogee bit.

11. Drill a 1"-diameter hole in the center of the top brace (D) to accommodate the dowel.

12. Screw the top brace to the spindle, then screw the top to the top brace. Glue can be used for extra reinforcement.

13. Finish the table as desired.

Also known as a candle stand table, this traditional favorite can be made quickly using a lathe. It lends itself to being a gift item as well.

1. Cut the stock to size according to the dimensions provided.

2. To make the template for the spindle (A), lay out the pattern on a piece of 1/4"-thick stock. Use a scroll saw, bandsaw, or jigsaw to cut out the pattern, and sand the edges smooth.

3. Mount the spindle stock on the lathe, turn the spindle, then sand. (If you glue up stock, it must be clamped for at least 24 hours before turning.)

4. Make a template for the legs (C) in the same manner, cut out the legs, and sand the curves on a drum sander.

5. Drill 3/8"-diameter holes to accommodate the dowels in the legs as shown.

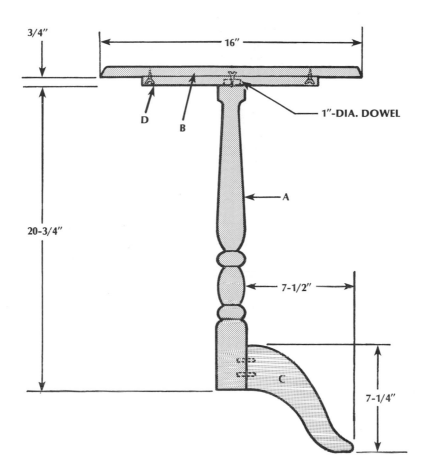

3/4"

16"

1"-DIA. DOWEL

D

B

A

20-3/4"

7-1/2"

C

7-1/4"

LIST OF MATERIALS

(finished dimensions in inches)

A	Spindle	2 dia. × 21-1/4
B	Top	3/4 × 16 dia.
C	Legs (3)	3/4 × 7-1/4 × 7-1/2
D	Top brace	3/4 × 3 × 12
	Wood screws	
	Dowels (10)	3/8 dia. × 1-1/2
	Wood glue	

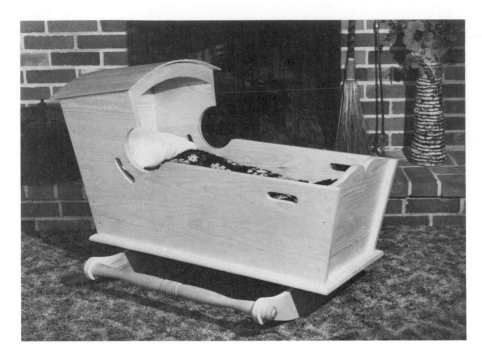

Hold it up to the assembled sides to mark the angles on the ends. Span the canopy support between the sides and secure it in place with glue and screws.

6. Attach the base to the bottom edge of the sides, headboard, and footboard with glue and counterbored screws from underneath.

7. Cut the canopy pieces (F, G) to size. While cutting to width, rip a 2° bevel on both edges of the center pieces and on the inner edge of each edge piece so the pieces form an arc as shown.

8. Starting in the center and working toward the ends, attach the canopy pieces with brads. When finished, sand the top for a smooth, rounded contour.

9. Cut two pieces of stock to 1-3/4″ × 1-3/4″ × 30″. Turn one treadle

Y ou'll love this old-fashioned cradle as much as your ancestors did. The lightly arched canopy protects a baby's sensitive eyes from harsh light. The convenient treadle bars allow you to rock the cradle with one foot while reading or knitting. In short, it's the perfect way to rock your child to sleep.

1. Use the patterns provided to cut the shapes of the sides (A), headboard (B), and footboard (C) to the dimensions provided. Cut the angle ends and bevel edges as shown.

2. Cut the handles in the sides, and shape the top edge of each piece as shown.

3. Shape the edge of the base (D) to the profile of your choice; the pattern shown is a radius bead. To minimize splintering, shape the ends of the base first, then do the sides.

4. Sand all of the pieces smooth. A drum sander will be necessary to sand the curve in the sides and the pattern cut in the footboard.

5. Assemble the sides to the headboard and footboard with glue and counterbored #8 × 1-1/2″ flathead wood screws. Transfer the pattern to the canopy support (E) stock.

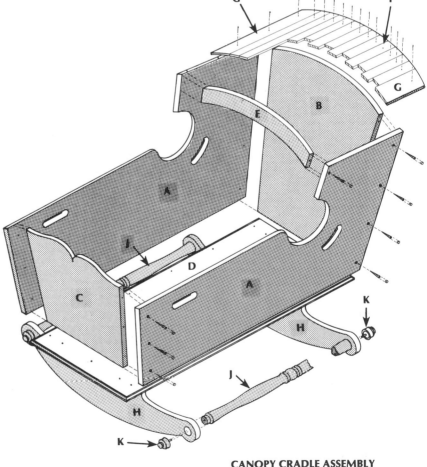

CANOPY CRADLE ASSEMBLY

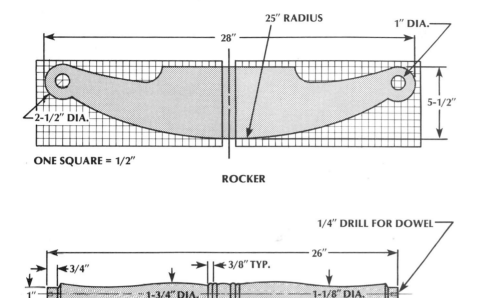

25" RADIUS

28"

1" DIA.

5-1/2"

2-1/2" DIA.

ONE SQUARE = 1/2"

ROCKER

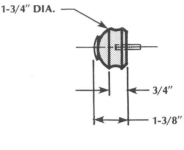

1-3/4" DIA.

3/4"

1-3/8"

END CAP

1/4" DRILL FOR DOWEL

3/4"

3/8" TYP.

26"

1-3/4" DIA.

1-1/8" DIA.

1"

11-1/2"

1"

1/4"

TREADLE BAR

bar (J) and two end caps (K) from each piece. Cut off the end caps and trim each piece to finished length.

10. Cut two pieces of stock to the listed dimensions for the rockers (H), then shape the pieces according to the pattern provided. Drill 1"-diameter holes in the rockers for the treadle bars.

11. Drill a 1/4"-diameter dowel hole 1/2" deep in each end of the treadle bars and in the adjoining end of each end cap.

12. Insert the ends of the treadle bars through the holes in the rockers. Attach the end caps with 1/4"-diameter × 1" dowels and glue. Then attach the rockers to the bottom of the base with glue and counterbored wood screws.

13. Cover all counterbored screws with 3/8"-diameter dowel plugs. Sand the plugs flush, then finish sand the cradle.

14. Finish as desired; a nontoxic finish is best. Make sure the finish is applied well in advance of the baby's arrival in order for the finish to dry and lose its odor. A polyurethane finish is best.

ONE SQUARE = 1/2"

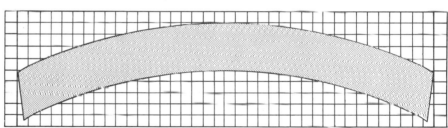

CANOPY SUPPORT PATTERN

LIST OF MATERIALS

(finished dimensions in inches)

A	Sides (2)	3/4 × 21-1/2 × 40
B	Headboard	3/4 × 23-1/4 × 19
C	Footboard	3/4 × 13-1/2 × 15-1/4
D	Base	3/4 × 15-1/2 × 36
E	Canopy support	3/4 × 4 × 19
F	Canopy center pieces (12)	1/4 × 1-1/4 × 14
G	Canopy edge pieces (2)	1/4 × 3 × 14
H	Rockers (2)	3/4 × 5-1/2 × 28
J	Treadle bars (2)	1-3/4 dia. × 26 dowels
K	End caps (4)	1-3/4 dia. × 1-3/8
	Dowels	1/4 dia. × 1
	Dowel plugs	3/8 dia. × 1/4
	Flathead wood screws	#8 × 1-1/2
	Brads	#18 × 1
	Wood glue	

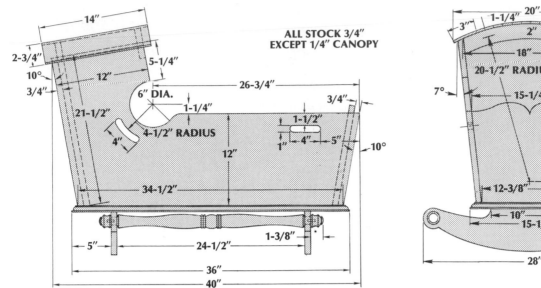

**ALL STOCK 3/4"
EXCEPT 1/4" CANOPY**

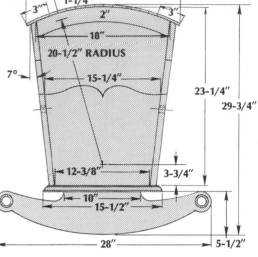

CANOPY CRADLE

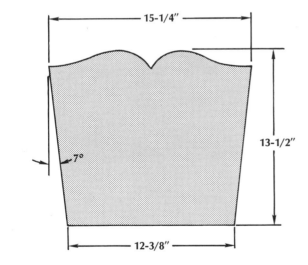

FOOTBOARD

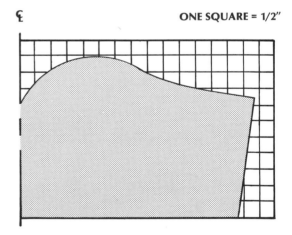

ONE SQUARE = 1/2"

TOP OF FOOTBOARD PATTERN

This coffee table can be built from clear grade redwood and features a tongue-and-groove board top. Feel free to use another variety of wood, either stained or left natural color.

1. Cut all of the pieces to size using the dimensions given.

2. Construct the inner legs (D, E) then connect them in two pairs by fastening a top support (H) to the backs of the wide inner leg pieces. The upper edge of the top supports should be flush with the top of the inner legs.

3. Fasten the outer legs (B, C) to the inner legs. To achieve a good corner joint, place a square block inside the inner legs and use band clamps to hold the assembly while it dries.

4. Set the side frame pieces (F) on the outer legs, their ends flush with the corner on the outer legs. Glue and nail in place, then fasten the end frame pieces (G) in position.

5. Rip one top piece (A) down the middle. Set the tongue section on the table and push its ripped edge against the side frame. Then fit the other three uncut pieces in place. Trim the ripped edge of the remaining piece as needed to fit it in and complete the top.

6. Make sure the outer pieces of the top are flush with the top of the side frames, then drive a few finishing nails through the frames into those top pieces. Also, drive nails through the ends of the top pieces into the top supports.

7. Turn the table over on its top. Fit the two cross braces (J) in place, then drive a couple of finishing nails through the side frames into the ends of each brace. Install glue blocks or metal corner bracing between the cross braces and the side frames.

8. Turn the table right side up and drive a pair of finishing nails through each full top piece, then drive one through each narrow piece into the brace.

9. Set all nails, fill the holes with putty, sand, and finish the table as desired.

LIST OF MATERIALS

(finished dimensions in inches)

A	Top pieces (4)	3/4 × 5-1/2 × 52-1/2 (tongue and groove)
B	Outer leg pieces (4)	3/4 × 3-1/2 × 12-1/2
C	Outer leg pieces (4)	3/4 × 2-1/2 × 12-1/2
D	Inner leg pieces (4)	3/4 × 2-1/2 × 17-1/4
E	Inner leg pieces (4)	3/4 × 1-1/2 × 17-1/4
F	Side frame pieces (2)	3/4 × 5-1/2 × 54
G	End frame pieces (2)	3/4 × 5-1/2 × 20-3/4
H	Top supports (2)	3/4 × 3-1/2 × 19-1/4
J	Cross braces (2)	1-1/2 × 3-1/2 × 20-3/4
	Wood screws	#8 × 1-1/4
	4d finishing nails	
	Glue blocks or metal corner bracing	
	Wood glue	

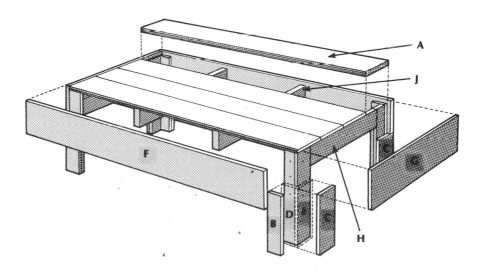

Index

CREDITS

Louisiana-Pacific Corp. (111 SW Fifth Avenue, Portland, Oregon, 97205): Corner Umbrella Stand; Cutting Board; Utensil Holder; Child's Easel; Christmas Ornaments; Workbench; Folding Tray.

Rodale Press, Inc. (33 E. Minor Street, Emmaus, Pennsylvania, 18098): Rocking Horse; Waddling Duck; Plant Shelf; Herb Drying Rack; Router Caddy.

Shopsmith® Inc. (3931 Image Drive, Dayton, Ohio, 45414): Magazine Rack; Recipe Box; Candelabra; Plant Display; Trivets; Watch Keep; Hanging Wine Glass Rack; Adjustable Plant Shelves; Candle Stands; Lap Tray and Coasters; African Marble Game; Toy Cars; Tugboat; Puzzles; Butcher Block Microwave Oven Stand; Sportsman's Rack; Chairside Bookcase; Armchair; Parsons Table; Triangular Table; Concord Table; Child's Cradle.

The Know Place. (4038-128 Avenue SE, Suite 176, Bellevue, Washington, 98009): Shoji Lamp; Plant Stand; Hall Tree; Stepladder Plant Stand; Gardening Bench; Wine Bottle Rack; Twin Bed; Reading Table; End Table; Drop Table; Gateleg Table; Coffee Table.